Python for Data Science:

A Crash Course for Data Science and Analysis, Python Machine Learning and Big Data

© **Copyright 2019 - All rights reserved.**

The content contained within this book may not be reproduced, duplicated or transmitted without direct written permission from the author or the publisher.

Under no circumstances will any blame or legal responsibility be held against the publisher, or author, for any damages, reparation, or monetary loss due to the information contained within this book. Either directly or indirectly.

Legal Notice:

This book is copyright protected. This book is only for personal use. You cannot amend, distribute, sell, use, quote or paraphrase any part, or the content within this book, without the consent of the author or publisher.

Disclaimer Notice:

Please note the information contained within this document is for educational and entertainment purposes only. All effort has been executed to present accurate, up to date, and reliable, complete information. No warranties of any kind are declared or implied. Readers acknowledge that the author is not engaging in the rendering of legal, financial, medical or professional advice. The content within this book has been derived from various sources. Please consult a licensed professional before attempting any techniques outlined in this book.

By reading this document, the reader agrees that under no circumstances is the author responsible for any losses, direct or indirect, which are incurred as a result of the use of information contained within this document, including, but not limited to, — errors, omissions, or inaccuracies.

Table of Content

Python for Data Science: 1

Table of Content 4

Introduction 6

Chapter 1: Foundational Data Science Technologies 9

    Data Science Lifecycle 11

        Standardized Project Structure... 12

        Infrastructure and Resources for Data Science Projects.... 14

        Tools and Utilities for Project Execution............................ 14

    Stage I – Business Understanding 16

    Stage II – Data Acquisition and Understanding 20

    Stage III – Modeling 22

    Stage IV – Deployment 25

    Stage V – Customer Acceptance 26

    Types of Data 28

    Data Science Strategies... 30

    Data Science vs Data Analysis 32

    Data Science in Cyber Security 33

Chapter 2: Introduction to Python Coding 36

    Installation Instructions for Python....................................... 37

    Python Variables 44

Python Data Types 46

Python Numbers 50

Python Strings... 55

Python Booleans... 64

Python Lists... 67

Python Tuples... 78

Python Sets... 85

Python Dictionary 92

Python Classes and Objects 106

Chapter 3: Data Visualization and Analysis with Python 120

Chapter 4: Machine Learning and Predictive Analysis............ 153

Conclusion.. 176

Introduction

Congratulations on purchasing *Python for Data Science: A Python Crash Course for Data Science, Data Analysis, Python Machine Learning and Big Data* and thank you for doing so.

The following chapters will discuss the fundamental concepts of Data Science driven by the Python programming language to provide you a holistic understanding of all the latest cutting edge technologies. In the first chapter, you will learn the basics of data science technology with an in-depth overview of the most widely used data science lifecycle called Team Data Science Process (TDSP). The five major stages of the TDSP lifecycle that outline the interactive steps required for project execution have been described from start to finish along with the deliverables created at each stage. To help you build a solid understanding of various technologies, the core concept of different types of data has been described with examples. The difference between the process of data analysis and data science has also been provided to avoid any confusion between them as these terms are often used interchangeably.

Chapter 2, entitled "Introduction to Python Coding," will help you master this extremely intuitive and flexible programming language that can be used for a variety of coding projects, including machine learning algorithms, web applications, data mining and visualization, game development. With the provide installation instructions for Python, you will be able to download and install Python on your operating system and get hands-on code development experience. Some of the Python coding concepts described in this chapter include data types, variables, numbers, constructor functions, strings, Booleans, classes and objects among others. Each concept is explained with examples and exercises so you can learn and test your learning at the same time.

Chapter 3, entitled "Data Visualization and Analysis with Python," deals with the concept of big data analytics and the functioning of big data. The different steps involved in big data analysis are explained in detail. The terms data analysis and data visualization are increasingly being used synonymously but this book will help you understand the distinction between the two with the use and application of some of the most popular Python-based libraries. Scikit-Learn has evolved as the gold standard for machine learning and data analysis with Matplotlib offering visualization tools and science computing modules supported by SciPy. You will learn how to create various graphs using matplotlib and Pandas library.

The final chapter of this book explores the concepts of machine learning and predictive analysis. Machine learning allows the analysis of large volumes of data and delivers faster and more accurate results. There are four different machine learning algorithms that can be used to cater to the available data set and create a desired machine learning model. A variety of real life examples of the application of machine learning technology have been provided to help you understand the importance of machine learning in the modern world. Today companies are digging through their past with an eye on the future and this is where artificial intelligence for marketing comes into play, with the application of predictive analytics technology. This chapter will provide you explicit details on how companies are able to employ a predictive analytics model to gain an understanding of how their customers are interacting with their products or services based on their feelings or emotions shared on the social media platforms.

There are plenty of books on this subject on the market, thanks again for choosing this one! Every effort was made to ensure it is full of as much useful information as possible; please enjoy!

Chapter 1: Foundational Data Science Technologies

In the world of technology, Data is defined as "information that is processed and stored by a computer." Our digital world has flooded our realities with data. From a click on a website to our smart phones tracking and recording our location every second of the day, our world is drowning in the data. From the depth of this humongous data, solutions to our problems that we have not even encountered yet could be extracted. This very process of gathering insights from a measurable set of data using mathematical equations and statistics can be defined as "data science." The role of data scientists tends to be very versatile and is often confused with a computer scientist and a statistician. Essentially anyone, be it a person or a company that is willing to dig deep to large volumes of data to gather information, can be referred to us data science practitioners. For example, companies like Walmart keeps track of and record of in-store and online purchases made by the customers, to provide personalized recommendations on products and services. The social media platforms like Facebook that allow users to list their current location is capable of identifying global migration patterns by analyzing the wealth of data that is handed to them by the users themselves.

The earliest recorded use of the term data science goes back to 1960 and credited to "Peter Naur," who reportedly used the term data science as a substitute for computer science and eventually introduced the term "datalogy." In 1974, Naur published a book titled "Concise Survey of Computer Methods," with liberal use of the term data science throughout the book. In 1992, the contemporary definition of data science was proposed at "The Second Japanese-French Statistics Symposium," with the acknowledgment of emergence of a new discipline focused primarily on types, dimensions and structures of data.

"Data science continues to evolve as one of the most promising and in-demand career paths for skilled professionals. Today, successful data professionals understand that they must advance past the traditional skills of analyzing large amounts of data, data mining, and programming skills. In order to uncover useful intelligence for their organizations, data scientists must master the full spectrum of the data science life cycle and possess a level of flexibility and understanding to maximize returns at each phase of the process."
– University of California, Berkley

An increasing interest by business executives has significantly contributed to the recent rise in popularity of the term data science. However, a large number of journalists and academic experts, do not acknowledge data science as a separate area of study from the field of statistics. A group within the same community considers data science is the popular term for "data mining" and "big data." The very definition of data science is up for debate within the tech community. The field of study that requires a combination of skill set including computer programming skills, domain expertise, and proficiency in statistics and mathematical algorithms to be able to extract valuable insight from large volumes of raw data is referred to as data science.

Data Science Lifecycle

The most highly recommended lifecycle to structured data science projects, the "Team Data Science Process" (TDSP). This process is widely used for projects that require the deployment of applications based on artificial intelligence and/or machine learning algorithms. It can also be customized for and used in the execution of "exploratory data science" projects as well as "ad hoc analytics" projects. The TDSP lifecycle is designed as an agile and sequential iteration of steps that serve as guidance on the tasks required for the use of predictive models. These predictive models need to be deployed in the production environment of the company, so they can be used in the development of artificial intelligence based applications. The aim of this data science lifecycle is high speed delivery and completion of data science projects toward a defined engagement end point. Seamless execution of any data science project requires effective communication of tasks within the team as well as to the stakeholders.

The fundamental components of the "Team Data Science Process" are:

Definition of a data science lifecycle
The five major stages of the TDSP lifecycle that outline the interactive steps required for project execution from start to finish are: "Business understanding," "Data acquisition in understanding," "modeling," "deployment" and "customer acceptance." Keep reading for details on this to come shortly!

Standardized Project Structure

To enable seamless and easy access to project documents for the team members allowing for quick retrieval of information, use of templates, and a shared directory structure goes a long way. All project documents and the project code our store and a "version control system" such as "TFS," "Git" or "Subversion" for improved team collaboration. Business requirements and associated tasks and functionalities are stored in an agile project tracking system like "JIRA," "Rally" and "Azure DevOps" to enable enhanced tracking of code for every single functionality. These tools also help in the estimation of resources and costs involved through the project lifecycle. To ensure effective management of each project, information security and team collaboration, TDSP confers the creation of separate storage for each project on the version control system. The adoption of a standardized structure for all the projects within an organization aid in the creation of an institutional knowledge library across the organization.

The TDSP lifecycle provides standard templates for all the required documents as well as folder structure at a centralized location. The files containing programming codes for the data exploration and extraction of the functionality can be organized to using the provided a folder structure, which also holds records pertaining to model iterations. These templates allow the team members to easily understand the work that has been completed by others as well as for a seamless addition of new team members to a given project. The markdown format supports ease of accessibility as well as making edits or updates to the document templates. To make sure the project goal and objectives are well defined and also to ensure the expected quality of the deliverables, these templates provide various checklists with important questions for each project. For example, a "project charter" can be used to document the project scope and the business problem that is being resolved by the project; standardized data reports are used to document the "structure and statistics" of the data.

Infrastructure and Resources for Data Science Projects

To effectively store infrastructure and manage shared analytics, the TDSP recommends using tools like: "machine learning service," databases, "big data clusters," and cloud based systems to store data sets. The analytics and storage infrastructure that houses raw as well as processed or cleaned data sets can be cloud-based or on-premises. D analytics and storage infrastructure permits the reproducibility of analysis and prevents duplication and the redundancy of data that can created inconsistency and unwarranted infrastructure costs. Tools are supplied to grant specific permissions to the shared resources and to track their activity, which in turn allows secure access to the resources for each member of the team.

Tools and Utilities for Project Execution

The introduction of any changes to an existing process tends to be rather challenging in most organizations. To encourage and raise the consistency of adoption of these changes, several tools can be implemented that are provided by the TDSP. Some of the basic tasks in the data science lifecycle including "data exploration" and "baseline modeling" can be easily automated with the tools provided by TDSP. To allow hassle free contribution of shared tools and utilities into the team's "shared code repository," TDSP from provides a well defined structure. This results in cost savings by allowing other project teams within the organization to reuse and repurpose these shared tools and utilities.

The TDSP lifecycle serves as a standardized template with a well-defined set of artifacts that can be used to garner effective team collaboration and communication across the board. This lifecycle is comprised of a selection of the best practices and structures from "Microsoft" to facilitated successful delivery predictive analytics Solutions and intelligent applications.

Let's look at the details of each of the five stages of the TDSP lifecycle, namely, "Business understanding," "Data acquisition in understanding," "modeling," "deployment" and "customer acceptance."

Data Science Lifecycle

Stage I – Business Understanding

The goal of this stage is to gather and drill down on the essential variables that will be used as targets for the model, and the metrics associated with these variables will ultimately determine the overall success of the project. Another significant objective of this stage is the identification of required data sources that the company already has or may need to procure. At this stage, the two primary tasks that are required to be accomplished are: "defining objects and identifying data sources."

Defining objectives

All projects must always start with the identification of the key business variables that the analytical tools are required to predict. These variables are called "model targets," and the metrics associated with these model targets, such as sales forecast and prediction of fraudulent orders, are used as a measure of the success of the project. To define the project goals and objectives, it is imperative to work with the stakeholders and the end users and asking relevant questions that can be highly specific or even vague. To answer these questions, the data science approach employs names and numbers. The five types of questions that are primarily used for data science or machine learning are pertaining to: "regression (how much or how many?), classification (what categories?), clustering (which groups?), anomaly detection (is this unusual?), recommendation (which option should be taken?)". It is important to determine the right questions for your project and understand how the answers to these questions will help you accomplish the business or project goals.

Specification and alignment of the roles and responsibilities of each member within the project team is quintessential to the success of the project. This can be accomplished with the help of a high level project plan containing significant milestones that can be modified as needed to the course of the project. Another important definition that should be agreed upon at this stage of the project is that all of the key performance indicators and metrics. For example, a project for prediction of customer turnover rate requiring the accuracy rate of "ABC" percent by the completion of the project can help you understand the requirement that must be fulfilled to meet the success criteria of the project. So in order to achieve the "ABC" percent accuracy rate, the company may run discount offers and promotions. The industry wide standard used in the development of metrics is called "SMART," which stands for "Specific, Measurable, Achievable, Relevant, Time bound."

Identification of data sources

The data sources that may contain "known examples" of answers to the five types of questions raised during the defining phase must be identified and accounted for. You must look for data that is in direct relevance to the questions asked and assess if you have a measurable target and features related to those targets. The data that serves as an accurate measure for the model target and its features is crucial for the determination of the project's success. For example, you might encounter a situation where the existing system is unable to collect and record the types of data that are required to accomplish the project goals. This should immediately inform you that you need to start looking for external data sources or run a system update to enable the collection of additional data types by the existing system.

Deliverables to be created in this stage

- **Charter document** – It is a "living document" that needs to be updated throughout the course of the project, in light of new project discoveries and changing business requirements. A standard template is supplied with the TDSP "project structure definition." It is important to build upon this document by adding more details throughout the course of the project while keeping the stakeholders promptly updated on all changes made.
- **Data sources** – Within the TDSP "project data report folder," the data sources can be found within the "Raw Data Sources" section of the "Data Definitions Report." The "Raw Data Sources" section also specifies the initial and final locations of the raw data and provide additional details like the "coding scripts" to move up the data to any desired environment.
- **Data dictionaries** – The descriptions of the characteristics and features of the data such as the "data schematics" and available "entity relationship diagrams," provided by the stakeholders are documented within the Data dictionaries.

Stage II – Data Acquisition and Understanding

The goal of this stage is the production of high quality processed data set with defined relationships to the model targets and location of the data set in the required analytics environment. At this stage, the "solution architecture" of the data pipeline must also be developed, which will allow regular updates to and scoring of the data. The three primary tasks that must be completed during this stage are: "Data ingestion, Data exploration and Data pipeline set up."

Data ingestion

The process required to transfer the data from the source location to the target location should be set up in this phase. The target locations are determined by the environments that will allow you to perform analytical activities like training and predictions.

Data exploration

The data set must be scrubbed to remove any discrepancies and errors before it can be used to train the Data models. To check the data quality and gathered information required to process the data before modeling, tools such as data summarization and visualization should be used. Since this process is repeated multiple times, an automated utility called "IDEAR," which is provided by TDSP can be used for Data visualization and creation of Data summary reports. With the achievement of satisfactory quality of the processed data, the inherent data patterns can be observed. This, in turn, helps in the selection and development of an appropriate "predictive model" for the target. Now you must assess if you have the required amount of data to start the modeling process, which is iterative in nature and may require you to identify new data sources to achieve higher relevance and accuracy.

Set up a data pipeline

To supplement the iterative process of data modeling, a standard process for scoring new data and refreshing the existing data set must be established by setting up a "data pipeline or workflow." The solution architecture of the data pipeline must be developed by the end of this stage. There are three types of pipelines that can be used on the basis of the business needs and constraints of the existing system: "batch based," "real-time or streaming," and "hybrid."

Deliverables to be created in this stage

- **Data quality report** – This report must include a "data summary" relationship between the business requirement and its attributes and variable ranking among other details. The "IDEAR" tool supplied with TDSP it's capable of generating data quality reports on a relational table, CSV file, or any other tabular data set.
- **Solution architecture** – A description or a diagram of the data pipeline that is used to score new data and generated predictions, after the model has been built can be referred to as "solution architecture." This diagram can also provide the data pipeline needed to "retrain" the model based on new data.
- **Checkpoint decision** –Prior to that start of the actual model building process project must be reevaluated to determine if the expected value can be achieved by pursuing the project. These are also called "Go or No-Go" decisions.

Stage III – Modeling

The goal of this stage is to find "optimal data features" for the machine learning model, which is informative enough to predict the target variables accurately and can be deployed in the production environment. The three primary tasks that must be accomplished in this stage are: "feature engineering, model training, and the determination of the suitability of the model for the production environment."

Feature engineering

The data features must be created from the raw data variables using the process of "inclusion, aggregation, and transformation." To be able to understand the functioning of the model, a clear understanding of how these data features relate to one another as well as to the machine learning algorithms that will be using those features must be developed. The insights gathered from the data exploration phase can be combined with domain expertise to allow creative feature engineering. The fine act of determining and including informative variables while making sure a whole lot of unrelated variables are not included in the data set is referred to as feature engineering. Too many unrelated variables will add noise to the data model, so an attempt must be made to add as many informative variables as possible to get better results. The features must also be generated for any new data collected doing the scoring.

Model training

A wide variety of modeling algorithms are available in the market today. The algorithm that meets the criteria of your project must be selected. The process for "model training" can be divided into four steps which are:

1. Creation of a "training data set" as well as a "test data set" by appropriately dividing the input data.
2. Development of the model with the use of the "training data set."
3. Evaluation of the training and the test data set, by employing various machine learning algorithms as well as related "tuning parameters" that are designed to help answer the previously discussed five types of questions from the existing data set.
4. Assess the best fit for the solution to resolve the business problem by comparing all available methods using key performance indicators and metrics.

TDSP provides an "automated modeling and reporting tool" that is capable of running through multiple algorithms and "parameters sweeps" to develop a "baseline model" as well as a "baseline modeling report" that can serve as a performance summary for each "model and parameter combination."

Deliverables to be created in this stage

- **Feature sets** – The document containing all the features described in the "feature sets section of the data definition report." It is heavily used by the programmers to write the

required code and develop features based on the basis of the description provided by the document.
- **Model report** – This document must contain the details of each model that was evaluated based on a standard template report.
- **Checkpoint decisions** – A decision regarding deployment of the model to the production environment must be made on the basis of the performance of different models.

Stage IV – Deployment

The goal of this stage is to release the solution models to a lower production like environments such as pre-production environment and user acceptance testing environment before eventually deploying the model in the production environment. The primary task to be accomplished in this stage is "operationalization of the model."

Operationalize the model

Once you have obtained a set of models with expected performance levels, these models can then be operationalized for other applicable applications to use. According to the business requirements, predictions can be made in real-time or on a batch basis. In order to deploy the model, they must be integrated with an open "Application Programming Interface" (API) to allow interaction of the model with all other applications and its components, as needed.

Deliverables to be created in this stage

- A dashboard report using the key performance indicators and metrics to access the health of the system.
- A document or run book with the details of the deployment plan for the final model.
- A document containing the solution architecture of the final model.

Stage V – Customer Acceptance

The goal of this stage is to ensure that the final solution for the project meets the expectations of the stakeholders and fulfills the business requirements gathered during Stage I of the Data science lifecycle. The two primary tasks that must be accomplished in this stage are: "system validation and project hand-off."

System validation – The final solution that will be deployed in the production environment must be evaluated against the business requirements and the data pipeline to make sure that the stakeholders needs are met. The stakeholder must validate that the system meets their business needs and resolves the problem that started the project in the first place. All the documentation must be thoroughly reviewed and finalized by the end of this stage.

Project hand-off – At this stage, the project must be transferred from the development team to the post production and maintenance team. For example, IT support team or someone from the stakeholder's team dad will provide day-to-day support for the solution in the production environment.

Deliverables to be created in this stage

The most important document created during this stage is for the stakeholders and called an "exit report." The document contains all of the available details of the project that are significant to provide an understanding of the operations of the system. TDSP supplies a standardized template for the "exit report," that can be easily customized to cater to specific stakeholder needs.

Types of Data

Now that you understand the importance of data science let us look at different types of data so you can choose the most appropriate analytical tools and algorithms is on the type of data that needs to be processed. Data types can be divided into two at a very high level: qualitative and quantitative.

Qualitative data – Any data that cannot be measured and only observed subjectively by adding a qualitative feature to the object it's called as "qualitative data." Classification of an object using unmeasurable features results in the creation of qualitative data. For example, attributes like color, smell, texture and taste. There are three types of qualitative data:

"Binary or binomial data" – Data values that signal mutually exclusive events where only one of the two categories or options is correct and applicable. For example, true or false, yes or no, positive or negative. Consider a box of assorted tea bags. You try all the different flavors and group the ones that you like as "good" and the ones you don't as "bad." In this case, "good or bad" would be categorized as binomial data type. This type of data is widely used in the development of statistical models for predictive analysis.

"**Nominal or unordered data**" – Data characteristics that lack an "implicit or natural value" can be referred to as nominal data. Consider a box of M&Ms, you can record the color of each M&M in the box in a worksheet, and that would serve as nominal data. This kind of data is widely used to assess statistical differences in the data set, using techniques like "Chi Square analysis," which could tell you "statistically significant differences" in the amount of each color of M&M in a box.

"**Ordered or ordinal data**" – The characteristics of this Data type do have certain "implicit or natural of value" such as small, medium, or large. For example, online reviews on the sites like "Yelp," "Amazon," and "Trip Advisor" have a rating scale from 1 to 5, implying 5 star rating is better than 4, which is better than 3 and so on.

Quantitative data – Any characteristics of the data that can be measured objectively are called as "quantitative data." Classification of an object in using measurable features and giving it a numerical value results and creation of quantitative data. For example, product prices, temperature, dimensions like length etc. There are two types of quantitative data:

"**Continuous Data**" – Data values that can be defined to a further lower level, such as units of measurement like kilometers, meters, centimeters, and on and on, are called as continuous data type. For example, you can purchase a bag of almonds by weight like 500 g or 8 ounces. This accounts for continuous data type, which is primarily used to test and verify different kinds of hypotheses such as assessing the accuracy of the weight printed on the bag of almonds.

"Discrete Data" – numerical data value that cannot be divided and reduced to a higher level of precision, such as the number of cars owned by a person which can only be accounted for as indivisible numbers (you cannot have 1.5 or 2.3 cars), is called as discrete data types. For example, you can purchase another bag of ice cream bars by the number of ice cream bars inside the package, like four or six. This accounts for the discrete data type, which can be used in combination with continuous data type to perform a regression analysis to verify if the total weight of the ice cream box (continuous data) is correlated with the number of ice cream bars (discrete data) inside.

Data Science Strategies

Data science is mainly used in decision-making by making precise predictions with the use of "predictive causal analytics," "prescriptive analytics," and machine learning.

Predictive causal analytics – The "predictive causal analytics" can be applied to develop a model that can accurately predict and forecast the likelihood of a particular event occurring in the future. For example, financial institutions use predictive causal analytics based tools to assess the likelihood of a customer defaulting on their credit card payments, by generating a model that can analyze the payment history of the customer with all of their borrowing institutions.

Prescriptive analytics - The "prescriptive analytics" are widely used in the development of "intelligent tools and applications" that are capable of modifying and learning with dynamic parameters and make their own "decisions." The tool not only predicts the occurrence of a future event but is also capable of providing recommendations on a variety of actions and its resulting outcomes. For example, the self-driving cars gather driving related data with every driving experience and use it to train themselves to make better driving and maneuvering decisions.

Machine learning to make predictions – To develop models that can determine future trends based on the transactional data acquired by the company, machine learning algorithms are a necessity. This is considered as "supervised machine learning," which we will elaborate on later in this book. For example, fraud detection systems use machine learning algorithms on the historical data pertaining to fraudulent purchases to detect if a transaction is fraudulent.

Machine learning for pattern discovery – To be able to develop models that are capable of identifying hidden data patterns but lack required parameters to make future predictions, the "unsupervised machine learning algorithms," such as "Clustering," need to be employed. For example, telecom companies often use the "clustering" technology to expand their network by identifying network tower locations with optimal signal strength in the targeted region.

Data Science vs Data Analysis

The terms of data science and data analytics are often used interchangeably. However, these terms are completely different and have different implications for different businesses. Data science encompasses a variety of scientific models and methods that can be used to manipulate and analyze structured, semi structured, and unstructured data. Tools and processes that can be used to make sense of gather insight from highly complex, unorganized and raw data set falls under the umbrella of data science. Unlike data analytics that is targeted to verify a hypothesis, data science boils down to connecting data points to identify new patterns and insights that can be made use of in future planning for the business. Data science moves the business from inquiry to insights by providing a new perspective into their structured and unstructured data by identifying patterns that can allow businesses to increase efficiencies, reduce costs and recognize the new market opportunities.

Data science acts as a multidisciplinary blend of technology, machine learning algorithm development, statistical analysis, and data inference that provides businesses with enhanced capability to solve their most complex business problems. Data analytics falls under the umbrella of data science and pertains more to reviewing and analyzing historical data to put it in context. Unlike data science, data analytics is characterized by low usage of artificial intelligence, predictive modeling and machine learning algorithms to gather insights from processed and structured data using standard SQL query commands. The seemingly nuanced differences between data analytics and data science can actually have a substantial impact on an organization.

Data Science in Cyber Security

The ability to analyze and closely examine Data trends and patterns using Machine learning algorithms has resulted in the significant application of data science in the cyber security space. With the use of data science, companies are not only able to identify the specific network terminal(s) that initiated the cyber-attack but are also in a position to predict potential future attacks on their systems and take required measures to prevent the attacks from happening in the first place. Use of "active intrusion detection systems" that are capable of monitoring users and devices on any network of choice and flag any unusual activity serves as a powerful weapon against hackers and cyber attackers. While the "predictive intrusion detection systems" that are capable of using machine learning algorithms on historical data to detect potential security threats serves as a powerful shield against the cyber predators.

Cyber-attacks can result in a loss of priceless data and information resulting in extreme damage to the organization. To secure and protect the data set, sophisticated encryption and complex signatures can be used to prevent unauthorized access. Data science can help with the development of such impenetrable protocols and algorithms. By analyzing the trends and patterns of previous cyber-attacks on companies across different industrial sectors, Data science can help detect the most frequently targeted data set and even predict potential future cyber-attacks. Companies rely heavily on the data generated and authorized by their customers but in the light of increasing cyber-attacks, customers are extremely wary of their personal information being compromised and are looking to take their businesses to the companies that are able to assure them of their data security and privacy by implementing advanced data security tools and technologies. This is where data science is becoming the saving grace of the companies by helping them enhance their cyber security measures.

Chapter 2: Introduction to Python Coding

Python was first implemented in 1989 and is regarded as highly user-friendly and simple to learn programming language for entry level coders and amateurs. It is a high-level programming language, commonly used for general purposes. It was originally developed by Guido van Rossum at the "Center Wiskunde & Informatica (CWI), Netherlands," in the 1980s and introduced by the "Python Software Foundation" in 1991. It was designed primarily to emphasize the readability of programming code, and its syntax enables programmers to convey ideas using fewer lines of code. Python programming language increases the speed of operation while allowing for higher efficiency in creating system integrations. It is regarded as ideal for individuals newly interested in programming or coding and needs to comprehend programming fundamentals. This stems from the fact that Python reads almost the same as English language. Therefore, it requires less time to understand how the language works and focus can be directed in learning the basics of programming.

Python is an interpreted language that supports automatic memory management and object-oriented programming. This extremely intuitive and flexible programming language can be used for coding projects such as machine learning algorithms, web applications, data mining and visualization, game development.

Installation Instructions for Python

Follow the s instructions below to download and install Python on your operating system by referring to the relevant section. The latest version of Python released in the middle of 2019 is Python 3.8.0. Make sure to download and install the most recent and stable version of Python at the time.

WINDOWS

1. From the official Python website, click on the "Downloads" icon and select Windows.
2. Click on the "Download Python 3.8.0" button to view all the downloadable files.
3. On subsequent screen, select the Python version you would like to download. In this book, we will be using the Python 3 version under "Stable Releases." So scroll down the page and click on the "Download Windows x86-64 executable installer" link, as shown in the picture below.

- Python 3.8.0 - Oct. 14, 2019
  Note that Python 3.8.0 *cannot* be used on Windows XP or earlier.
  - Download Windows help file
  - Download Windows x86-64 embeddable zip file
  - Download Windows x86-64 executable installer
  - Download Windows x86-64 web-based installer
  - Download Windows x86 embeddable zip file
  - Download Windows x86 executable installer
  - Download Windows x86 web-based installer

4. A pop up window titled "python-3.8.0-amd64.exe" will be shown.
5. Click on the "Save File" button to start downloading the file.
6. Once the download has completed, double click the saved file icon, and a "Python 3.8.0 (64-bit) Setup" pop window will be shown.
7. Make sure that you select the "Install Launcher for all users (recommended)" and the "Add Python 3.8 to PATH" checkboxes. Note – If you already have an older version of Python installed on your system, the "Upgrade Now" button will appear instead of the "Install Now" button, and neither of the checkboxes will be shown.
8. Click on "Install Now" and a "User Account Control" pop up window will be shown.
9. A notification stating, "Do you want to allow this app to make changes to your device" will be shown, click on Yes.
10. A new pop up window titled "Python 3.8.0 (64-bit) Setup" will be shown containing a setup progress bar.

11. Once the installation has been completed, a "Set was successful" message will be shown. Click on Close.
12. To verify the installation, navigate to the directory where you installed Python and double click on the python.exe file.

MACINTOSH

1. From the official Python website, click on the "Downloads" icon and select Mac.
2. Click on the "Download Python 3.8.0" button to view all the downloadable files.
3. On the subsequent screen, select the Python version you would like to download. In this book, we will be using the Python 3 version under "Stable Releases." So scroll down the page and click on the "Download macOS 64-bit installer" link under Python 3.8.0, as shown in the picture below.

- Python 3.7.5 - Oct. 15, 2019
    - Download macOS 64-bit/32-bit installer
    - Download macOS 64-bit installer
- Python 3.8.0 - Oct. 14, 2019
    - Download macOS 64-bit installer
- Python 3.7.4 - July 8, 2019
    - Download macOS 64-bit/32-bit installer
    - Download macOS 64-bit installer
- Python 3.6.9 - July 2, 2019

4. A pop up window titled "python-3.8.0-macosx10.9.pkg" will be shown.
5. Click "Save File" to start downloading the file.
6. Once the download has completed, double click the saved file icon, and an "Install Python" pop window will be shown.
7. Click "Continue" to proceed, and the terms and conditions pop up window will appear.
8. Click Agree and then click "Install."
9. A notification requesting administrator permission and password will be shown. Enter your system password to start installation.
10. Once the installation has finished, an "Installation was successful" message will appear. Click on the Close button, and you are all set.
11. To verify the installation, navigate to the directory where you installed Python and double click on the python launcher icon that will take you to the Python Terminal.

LINUX

- **For Red Hat, CentOS, or Fedora**, install the python3 and python3-devel packages.
- **For Debian or Ubuntu**, install the python3.x and python3.x-dev packages.

- **For Gentoo**, install the '=python-3.x*' ebuild (you may have to unmask it first).

1. From the official Python website, click on the "Downloads" icon and select Linux/UNIX.
2. Click on the "Download Python 3.8.0" button to view all the downloadable files.
3. On subsequent screen, select the Python version you would like to download. In this book, we will be using the Python 3 version under "Stable Releases." So scroll down the page and click on the "Download Gzipped source tarball" link under Python 3.8.0, as shown in the picture below.

- Download Gzipped source tarball
- Download XZ compressed source tarball
- Python 3.8.0 - Oct. 14, 2019
    - Download Gzipped source tarball
    - Download XZ compressed source tarball
- Python 3.7.4 - July 8, 2019
    - Download Gzipped source tarball
    - Download XZ compressed source tarball

4. A pop up window titled "python-3.7.5.tgz" will be shown.
5. Click "Save File" to begin downloading the file.
6. Once the download has finished, double click the saved file icon, and an "Install Python" pop window will appear.
7. Follow the prompts on the screen to complete the installation process.

Getting Started

With the Python terminal installed on your computer, you can now start writing and executing the Python code. All Python codes are written in a text editor as (.py) files and executed on the Python interpreter command line as shown in the code below, where "nineplanets.py" is the name of the Python file:

"C: \Users\Your Name\python nineplanets.py"

You will be able to test a small code without writing it in a file and simply executing it as a command line itself by typing the code below on the Mac, Windows or Linux command line, as shown below:

"C: \Users\Your Name\python"

In case the command above does not work, use the code below instead:

"C: \Users\Your Name\py"

Indentation – The importance of indentation, which is the number of spaces preceding the code, is fundamental to the Python coding structure. In most programming languages, indentation is added to enhance the readability of the code. However, in Python, the indentation is used to indicate execution of a subset of the code, as shown in the code below

If 7 > 2:
   print ('Seven is greater than two')

Indentation precedes the second line of code with the print command. If the indentation is skipped and the code was written as below, an error will be triggered:

If 7 > 2:
print ('Seven is greater than two')

The number of spaces can be modified but is required to have at least one space. For example, you can execute the code below with higher indentation, but for a specific set of code same number of spaces must be used, or you will receive an error.

If 7 > 2:
      print ('Seven is greater than two')

Adding Comments – In Python, comments can be added to the code by starting the code comment lines with a "#," as shown in the example below:

#Any relevant comments will be added here
print ('Nine planets')

Comments serve as a description of the code and will not be executed by the Python terminal. Make sure to remember that any comments at the end of the code line will lead to the entire code line being skipped by the Python terminal, as shown in the code below. Comments can be very useful in case you need to stop the execution when you are testing the code.

print ('Nine Planets')   #Comments added here

Multiple lines of comments can be added by starting each code line with "#," as shown below:

#Comments added here

#Supplementing the comments here
#Further adding the comments here
print ('Nine Planets')

Python Variables

In Python, variables are primarily utilized to save data values without executing a command for it. A variable can be created by simply assigning the desired value to it, as shown in the example below:

A = 999
B = 'Patricia'
print (A)
print (B)

A variable could be declared without a specific data type. The data type of a variable can also be modified after it's an initial declaration, as shown in the example below:

A = 999 # A has data type set as int
A = 'Patricia' # A now has data type str
print (A)

Some of the rules applied to the Python variable names are as follows:

1. Variable names could be as short as single alphabets or more descriptive words like height, weight, and more.
2. Variable names could only be started with an underscore character or a letter.
3. Variable names must not start with numbers.
4. Variable names can contain underscores or alpha numeric characters. No other special characters are allowed.

5. Variable names are case sensitive. For example, 'weight,' 'Weight,' and 'WEIGHT' will be accounted as 3 separate variables.

Assigning Value to Variables

In Python, multiple variables can be assigned DISTINCT values in a single code line, as shown in the example below:

A, B, C = 'violet,' maroon, 'teal'
print (A)
print (B)
print (C)

OR multiple variables can be assigned SAME value in a single code line, as shown in the example below:

A, B, C = 'violet'
print (A)
print (B)
print (C)

Python Data Types

Python supports a variety of data types, as listed below. To build a solid understanding of the concept of variables, you must learn all the Python data types.

Category	Data Type	Example Syntax
Text	*"str"*	'Nine Planets' "Nine Planets" """"Nine Planets""""
Boolean	*"bool"*	'True' 'False'
Mapping (mixed data types, associative array of key and value pairs)	*"dict"*	'{'key8' : 8.0, 5 : True}'
Sequence (may contain mixed data types)	*"list"*	'[8.0, 'character', True]'
	"tuple"	'[8.0, 'character', True]'
	"range"	'range (11, 51)' 'range (110, 51, 11, -11, -51, -110)'
Binary	*"bytes"*	b 'byte sequences' b 'byte sequences' bytes ([121, 91, 75, 110])
	"bytearray"	bytearray (b 'byte sequences') bytearray (b 'byte sequences') bytearray ([121, 91. 75, 110])
	"memoryview"	

46

Set (unordered, no duplicates, mixed data types)	*"set"*	'[8.0, 'character', True]'
	"frozenset"	'frozenset ([8.0, 'character', True])'
Numeric	*"int"*	'35'
	"float"	'155e3'
	"complex"	'155 + 2.1j'
Ellipsis (index in NumPy arrays)	*"ellipsis"*	'...' 'Ellipsis'

To view the data type of any object, you can use the *"type ()"* function as shown in the example below:

A = 'Violet'
print (type (A))

Assigning the Data Type to Variables

A new variable can be created by simply declaring a value for it. This set data value will in turn assign the data type to the variable.

To assign a specific data type to a variable, the constructor functions listed below are used:

Constructor Functions	**Data Type**
A = str ('Nine Planets)'	str
A = int (55)	Int (Must be a whole number, positive or negative with no decimals, no length restrictions)
A = float (14e6)	Float (Floating point number must be positive or negative number with one or more

	decimals; maybe scientific number an 'e' to specify an exponential power of 10)
A = complex (92j)	Complex (Must be written with a 'j' as an imaginary character)
A = list (('teal', maroon, 'jade'))	list
A = range (3, 110)	range
A = tuple (('teal', maroon, 'jade'))	tuple
A = set (('teal', maroon, 'jade'))	set
A = frozenset (('teal', 'jade', maroon))	frozenset
A = dict ('color' : maroon, 'year' : 1988)	dict
A = bool (False)	bool
A = bytes (542)	bytes
A = bytearray (9)	bytearray
A = memoryview (bytes (525))	memoryview

EXERCISE – To solidify your understanding of data types. Look at the first column of the table below and write the data type for that variable. Once you have all your answers, look at the second column, and verify your answers.

Variable	Data Type
A = 'Nine Planets'	str
A = 45	int
A = 56e2	float
A = 34j	complex
A = ['teal', maroon, 'jade']	list
A = range (12, 103)	range
A = ('teal', maroon, 'jade')	tuple

A = {'teal', maroon, 'jade'}	set
A = frozenset ({ 'teal', 'jade', maroon})	frozenset
A = ['color' : maroon, 'year' : 1939}	dict
A = False	bool
A = b 'Morning'	bytes
A = bytearray (5)	bytearray
A = memoryview (bytes (45))	memoryview

Output Variables

In order to retrieve variables as output, the "print" statements are used in Python. You can use the "+" character to combine text with a variable for final output, as shown in the example below:

'A = maroon
print ('Flowers are' + A)'

OUTPUT – 'Flowers are maroon'

A variable can also be combined with another variable using the "+" character as shown in the example below:

'A = 'Flowers are'
B = maroon
AB = A + B
print (AB)'

OUTPUT – 'Flowers are maroon'

However, when the "+" character is used with numeric values, it retains its function as mathematical operator, as shown in the example below:

'A = 22
B = 33
print (A + B)'

OUTPUT = 55

You will not be able to combine a string of characters with numbers and will trigger an error instead, as shown in the example below:

A = yellow
B = 30
print (A + B)

OUTPUT – N/A – ERROR

Python Numbers

In Python programming, you will be working with 3 different numeric data types, namely, "int", "float" and "complex". In the previous chapter, you learned the details of what these data types entail, but below are some examples to refresh your memory.

Data Type	Example
Int (Must be a whole number, positive or negative with no decimals, no length restrictions)	*388 or 3.42*
Float (Floating point number must be a positive or negative number with one or more decimals; maybe scientific number an "e" to specify an exponential power of 10)	*41e4*
Complex (Must be written with a "j" as an imaginary character)	*46j*

EXERCISE – Create variable "a" with data value as "4.25", variable "b" with data value as "7e3" and variable "c" with data value as "-59j".

USE YOUR DISCRETION HERE AND WRITE YOUR CODE FIRST

Now, check your code against the correct code below:

```
a = 4.25      # int
b = 7e3       # float
c = -59j      # complex

print (type (a))
print (type (b))
print (type (c))
```

Note – The # comments are not required for the correct code and are only mentioned to bolster your understanding of the concept.

Converting one numeric data type to another

As all Python variables are dynamic in nature, you will be able to convert the data type of these variables if needed by deriving a new variable from the variable that you would like to assign a new data type.

Let's continue building on the exercise discussed above.

```
a = 4.25        # int
b = 7e3         # float
c = -49j        # complex

#conversion from int to float
x = float (a)

#conversion from float to complex
y = complex (b)

#conversion from complex to int
z = float (c)

#conversion from int to complex
x1 = int (a)

print (x)
print (y)
print (z)
print (x1)

print (type (x))
print (type (y))
```

print (type (z))

print (type (x1))

EXERCISE – View a random number between 11 and 21 by importing the random module.

USE YOUR DISCRETION HERE AND WRITE YOUR CODE FIRST

Now, check your code against the correct code below:

import random

print (random.randrange (11, 21))

Variable Casting with Constructor Functions

In the discussion and exercise above, you learned that variables can be declared by simply assigning desired data value to them and thereby, the variables will assume the pertinent data type based on the data value. However, Python allows you to specify the data types for variables by using classes or "constructor functions" to define the data type for variables. This process is called "Casting."

Here are the 3 constructor functions used for "casting" numeric data type to a variable.

Constructor Functions	Data Type
int ()	Will construct an integer number from an integer literal, a string literal (provided the string is representing a whole number) or a float literal (by rounding down to the preceding whole number)
float ()	Will construct a float number from a string literal (provided the string is representing a float or an integer), a float literal or an integer literal
complex ()	Will construct a string from a large number of data types, such as integer literals, float literals, and strings

Here are some examples:

Integer:

a = int (7)   # a takes the value 7
b = int (2.8)   # b takes the value 3
c = int ('6')   # c takes the value 6

Float:

54

a = float (7)   # a takes the value 7.0
b = float (2.8)   # b takes the value 2.8
c = float ('6')   # c takes the value 6.0

String:
a = str ('serial')   # a takes the value 'serial'
b = str (2.8)   # b takes the value '2.8'
c = str ('6')   # c takes the value '6.0'

Python Strings

In Python, string data type for a variable is denoted by using single, double, or triple quotation marks. This implies that you can assign string data value to variable by quoting the string of characters. For example, "welcome" is the same as 'welcome' and '"welcome"'.

EXERCISE – Create a variable "v" with a string data value as "I like teal" and display it.

USE YOUR DISCRETION HERE AND WRITE YOUR CODE FIRST

Now, check your code against the correct code below:

v = 'I like teal'
print (v)

OUTPUT – I like teal

EXERCISE – Create a variable "A" with a multiple line string data value as "Looking at the sky tonight, thinking of you by my side!
Let the world go on and on; it will be alright if I stay strong!" and display it.

USE YOUR DISCRETION HERE AND WRITE YOUR CODE FIRST***

Now, check your code against the correct code below:

a = '"Looking at the sky tonight,
thinking of you by my side!
Let the world go on and on,
it will be alright if I stay strong!"'
print (a)

OUTPUT – Looking at the sky tonight,
thinking of you by my side!
Let the world go on and on,
it will be alright if I stay strong!

Note – You must use triple quote to create multiline string data values.

String Arrays

In Python, string data values are arrays of bytes that represent Unicode characters as true for most programming languages. But unlike other programming languages, Python lacks data type for individual characters, which are denoted as string data type with length of 1.

The first character of every string is given the position of '0', and subsequently, the subsequent characters will have the position as 1, 2, 3, and so on. In order to display desired characters from a string data value, you can use the position of the character enclosed in square brackets. For example, if you wanted to display the fourth character of the string data value "cranberry" of variable "x." You will use the command "print (x [3])"

EXERCISE – Create a variable "P" with a string data value as "wonderful" and display the fifth character of this string.

USE YOUR DISCRETION HERE AND WRITE YOUR CODE FIRST

Now, check your code against the correct code below:

P = 'wonderful'
print (P [4])

OUTPUT – e

Slicing

If you would like to view a range of characters, you can do so by specifying the start and the end index of the desired positions and separating the indexes by a colon. For example, to view characters of a string from position 2 to position 5, your code will be *"print (variable [2:5])"*.

You can even view the characters starting from the end of the string by using "negative indexes" and start slicing the string from the end of the string. For example, to view characters of a string from position 3 to position 1, your code will be *"print (variable [-3 : -2])"*.

In order to view the length of the string, you can use the "len ()" function. For example, to view the length of a string, your code will be *"print (len (variable))."*

EXERCISE – Create a variable "P" with a string data value as "birds can sing!" and display characters from position 2 to 5 of this string.

USE YOUR DISCRETION HERE AND WRITE YOUR CODE FIRST

Now, check your code against the correct code below:

P = 'birds can sing!'
print (P [2 : 5])

OUTPUT – rdsc

EXERCISE – Create a variable "x" with a string data value as "coding is easy" and display characters from position 4 to 1, starting the count from the end of this string.

USE YOUR DISCRETION HERE AND WRITE YOUR CODE FIRST

Now, check your code against the correct code below:

x = 'coding is easy'
print (x [-4 : -2])

OUTPUT - ea

EXERCISE – Create a variable "z" with a string data value as "good morning" and display the length of this string.

USE YOUR DISCRETION HERE AND WRITE YOUR CODE FIRST

Now, check your code against the correct code below:

z = 'good morning'
print (len (z))

OUTPUT - 11

String Methods

There are various built-in methods in Python that can be applied to string data values. Here are the Python codes for some of the most frequently used string methods, using variable "P = 'birds can sing!'".

"strip ()" method – To remove any blank spaces at the start and the end of the string.

P = " birds can sing!   "

print (P.strip ())

OUTPUT – birds can sing!

"lower ()" method – To result in all the characters of a string in lower case.

P = "Birds can sing!"
print (P.lower ())

OUTPUT – birds can sing!

"upper ()" method – To result in all the characters of a string in upper case.

P = "Birds can sing!"
print (P.upper ())

OUTPUT – BIRDS CAN SING!

"replace ()" method – To replace select characters of a string.

P = "birds can sing!"
print (P.replace ("birds", "Songbirds"))

OUTPUT – Songbirds can sing!

"split ()" method – To split a string into substrings using comma as the separator.

P = "Birds, Songbirds"
print (P.split (","))

OUTPUT – ['Birds',   'Songbirds']

String Concatenation

There might be instances when you need to collate different string variables. This can be accomplished with the use of the "+" logical operator. Here's the syntax for this Python code:

X = "string1"
Y = "string2"
Z = X + Y
print (Z)

Similarly, below is the syntax to insert a blank space between two different string variables.

X = "string1"
Y = "string2"
Z = X + " " + Y
print (Z)

However, Python does not permit concatenation of string variables with numeric variables. But can be accomplished with the use of the *"format ()"* method, which will format the executed arguments and place them in the string where the placeholders "{ }" are used. Here's the syntax for this Python code:

X = numeric
Y = "String"
print (Y. format (X))

EXERCISE – Create two variables "A" and "B" with string data values as "The winter" and "is coming!" and display them as a concatenated string.

USE YOUR DISCRETION HERE AND WRITE YOUR CODE FIRST

Now, check your code against the correct code below:

A = "The winter"
B = "is coming!"
C = A + B
print (C)

OUTPUT – The winter is coming!

EXERCISE – Create two variables "A" with string data values as "her lucky number is" and "B" with numeric data value as "3333" and display them as a concatenated string.

USE YOUR DISCRETION HERE AND WRITE YOUR CODE FIRST

Now, check your code against the correct code below:

A = "her lucky number is"
B = "3333"
print (A. format (B))

OUTPUT – her lucky number is 3333

Python Booleans

In the process of developing a software program, there is often a need to confirm and verify whether an expression is true or false. This is where Python Boolean data type and data values are used. In Python, comparison and evaluation of two data values will result in one of the two Boolean values: "True" or "False".

Here are some examples of comparison statement of numeric data leading to Boolean value:

print (110 > 94)

OUTPUT – True

print (110 > 94)

OUTPUT – False

print (110 > 94)

OUTPUT – False

Let's look at the *"bool ()"* function now, which allows for evaluation of numeric data as well as string data resulting in "True" or "False" Boolean values.

print (bool (93))

OUTPUT - True

print (bool ("Welcome"))

OUTPUT - True

Here are some key points to remember for Booleans:

1. If a statement has some kind of content, it would be evaluated as "True".
2. All string data values will be result ined as "True" unless the string is empty.
3. All numeric values will be result ined as "True" except "0"
4. Lists, Tuples, Set and Dictionaries will be result ined as "True", unless they are empty.
5. Mostly empty values like (), [], {}, "", False, None and 0 will be result ined as "False".
6. Any object created with the "_len_" function that result in the data value as "0" or "False" will be evaluated as "False".

In Python there are various built-in functions function that can be evaluated as Boolean, for example, the "isinstance()" function which allows you to determine the data type of an object. Therefore, in order to check if an object is integer, the code will be as below:

X = 10
print (isinstance (X, int))

EXERCISE – Create two variables "X" with string data values as "Happy New Year!" and "Y" with numeric data value as "4.55" and evaluate them.

USE YOUR DISCRETION HERE AND WRITE YOUR CODE FIRST

Now, check your code against the correct code below:

X = "Happy New Year!"
Y = 4.55

print (bool (X))
print (bool (Y))

OUTPUT –
True
True

Python Lists

In Python, Lists are collections of data types that can be changed, organized and include duplicate values. Lists are written within square brackets, as shown in the syntax below.

X = ["string1", "string2", "string3"]
print (X)

The same concept of position applies to Lists as the string data type, which dictates that the first string is considered to be at position 0. Subsequently the strings that will follow are given position 1, 2, and so on. You can selectively display desired string from a List by referencing the position of that string inside square bracket in the print command as shown below.

X = ["string1", "string2", "string3"]
print (X [2])

OUTPUT – [string3]

Similarly, the concept of **negative indexing** is also applied to Python List. Let's look at the example below:

X = ["string1", "string2", "string3"]
print (X [-2])

OUTPUT – [string2]

You will also be able to specify a **range of indexes** by indicating the start and end of a range. The result in values of such command on a Python List would be a new List containing only the indicated items. Here is an example for your reference.

X = ["string1", "string2", "string3", "string4", "string5", "string6"]
print (X [3 : 5])

OUTPUT – ["string4", "string5"]

* Remember the first item is at position 0, and the final position of the range (4) is not included.

Now, if you do not indicate the start of this range, it will default to the position 0 as shown in the example below:

X = ["string1", "string2", "string3", "string4", "string5", "string6"]
print (X [: 4])

OUTPUT – ["string1", "string2", "string3" , "string4"]

Similarly, if you do not indicate the end of this range it will display all the items of the List from the indicated start range to the end of the List, as shown in the example below:

X = ["string1", "string2", "string3", "string4", "string5", "string6"]
print (X [4 :])

OUTPUT – ["string5", "string6"]

You can also specify a **range of negative indexes** to Python Lists, as shown in the example below:

X = ["string1", "string2", "string3", "string4", "string5", "string6"]

print (X [-4 : -1])

OUTPUT – ["string3", *"string4"*, "string5"]

* Remember the last item is at position -1, and the final position of this range (-1) is not included in the Output.

There might be instances when you need to **change the data value** for a Python List. This can be accomplished by referring to the index number of that item and declaring the new value. Let's look at the example below:

X = ["string1", "string2", "string3", "string4", "string5", "string6"]
X [2] = "newstring"
print (X)

OUTPUT – ["string1", "string2", "newstring", "string4", "string5", "string6"]

You can also determine the **length** of a Python List using the "len()" function, as shown in the example below:

X = ["string1", "string2", "string3", "string4", "string5"] print (len (X))

OUTPUT – 5

Python Lists can also be changed by **adding new items** to an existing List using the built-in "append ()" method, as shown in the example below:

X = ["string1", "string2", "string3", "string4", "string5"]
X.append ("newstring")
print (X)

OUTPUT – ["string1", "string2", "string3", "string4", "string5", "newstring"]

You can also, add a new item to an existing Python List at a specific position using the built-in "insert ()" method, as shown in the example below:

X = ["string1", "string2", "string3", "string4"]
X.insert (3, "newstring")
print (X)

OUTPUT – ["string1", "string2", "string3", "newstring"]

There might be instances when you need to **copy** an existing Python List. This can be accomplished by using the built-in "copy ( )" method or the "list ( )" method, as shown in the example below:

X = ["string1", "string2", "string3", "string4", "string5", "string6"]
Y = X.copy( )
print (Y)

OUTPUT – ["string1", "string2", "string3", "string4", "string5", "string6"]

X = ["string1", "string2", "string3", "string4", "string5", "string6"]
Y = list (X)
print (Y)

OUTPUT – ["string1", "string2", "string3", "string4", "string5", "string6"]

There are multiple built-in methods to **delete items** from a Python List.

- To selectively delete a specific item, the "remove ()" method can be used.

  X = ["string1", "string2", "string3", "string4"]

  X.remove ("string2")

  print (X)

  OUTPUT - ["string1", "string3", "string4"]

- To delete a specific item from the List, the "pop ()" method can be used with the position of the value. If no index has been indicated, the last item of the index will be removed.

  X = ["string1", "string2", "string3", "string4"]

  X.pop ( )

  print (X)

  OUTPUT - ["string1", "string2", "string3"]

- To delete a specific index from the List, the "del ()" method can be used, followed by the index within square brackets.

  X = ["string1", "string2", "string3", "string4"]

  del X [2]

  print (X)

  OUTPUT - ["string1", "string2", "string4"]

- To delete the entire List variable, the "del ()" method can be used, as shown below.

  X = ["string1", "string2", "string3", "string4"]

  del X

  OUTPUT - .....

- To delete all the string values from the List without deleting the variable itself, the "clear ()" method can be used, as shown below.

  X = ["string1", "string2", "string3", "string4"]

  X.clear()

  print (X)

  OUTPUT – [ ]

Concatenation of Lists

You can join multiple lists with the use of the "+" logical operator or by adding all the items from one list to another using the "append ( )" method. The "extend ( )" method can be used to add a list at the end of another list. Let's look at the examples below to understand these commands.

X = ["string1", "string2", "string3", "string4"]

Y = [11, 22, 33, 40]

Z = X + Y
print (Z)

OUTPUT – ["string1", "string2", "string3", "string4", 11, 22, 33, 40]

X = ["string1", "string2", "string3", "string4"]
Y = [11, 22, 33, 40]

For x in Y:
    X.append (x)

print (X)

OUTPUT – ["string1", "string2", "string3", "string4", 11, 22, 33, 40]

X = ["string1", "string2", "string3"]
Y = [11, 22, 33]

X.extend (Y)
print (X)

OUTPUT – ["string1", "string2", "string3", 11, 22, 33]

EXERCISE – Create a list "A" with string data values as "red, jade, teal, violet, yellow" and display the item at -2 position.

USE YOUR DISCRETION HERE AND WRITE YOUR CODE FIRST

Now, check your code against the correct code below:

A = ["red," "jade," "teal," "violet," "yellow"]
print (A [-2])

OUTPUT – ["violet"]

EXERCISE – Create a list "A" with string data values as "red, jade, teal, violet, yellow" and display the items ranging from the string on the second position to the end of the string.

USE YOUR DISCRETION HERE AND WRITE YOUR CODE FIRST

Now, check your code against the correct code below:

A = ["red," "jade," "teal," "violet," "yellow"]
print (A [2 :])

OUTPUT – ["red," "teal," "teal," "violet," "yellow"]

EXERCISE – Create a list "A" with string data values as "red, jade, teal, violet, yellow" and replace the string "jade" to "teal."

USE YOUR DISCRETION HERE AND WRITE YOUR CODE FIRST

Now, check your code against the correct code below:

A = ["red," "jade," "teal," "violet," "yellow"]
A [1] = ["teal"]

print (A)

OUTPUT – ["teal," "violet," "yellow"]

EXERCISE – Create a list "A" with string data values as "red, jade, teal, violet, yellow" and copy the list "A" to create list "B."

USE YOUR DISCRETION HERE AND WRITE YOUR CODE FIRST

Now, check your code against the correct code below:

A = ["red," "jade," "teal," "violet," "yellow"]
B = A.copy ( )

print (B)

OUTPUT – ["red," "jade," "teal," "violet," "yellow"]

EXERCISE – Create a list "A" with string data values as "red, jade, teal, violet, yellow" and delete the strings "red" and "violet."

USE YOUR DISCRETION HERE AND WRITE YOUR CODE FIRST

Now, check your code against the correct code below:

A = ["red," "jade," "teal," "violet," "yellow"]
del.A [0, 2]
print (A)

OUTPUT – ["jade," "teal," "yellow"]

Python Tuples

In Python, Tuples are collections of data types that cannot be changed but can be arranged in a specific order. Tuples allow for duplicate items and are written within round brackets, as shown in the syntax below.

Tuple = ("string1", "string2", "string3")
print (Tuple)

Similar to the Python List, you can selectively display the desired string from a Tuple by referencing the position of that string inside square bracket in the print command, as shown below.

Tuple = ("string1", "string2", "string3")
print (Tuple [1])

OUTPUT – ("string2")

The concept of **negative indexing** can also be applied to Python Tuple, as shown in the example below:
Tuple = ("string1", "string2", "string3", "string4", "string5")
print (Tuple [-2])

OUTPUT – ("string4")

You will also be able to specify a **range of indexes** by indicating the start and end of a range. The result in values of such command on a Python Tuple would be a new Tuple containing only the indicated items, as shown in the example below:

Tuple = ("string1", "string2", "string3", "string4", "string5", "string6") print (Tuple [1:5])

OUTPUT – *("string2", "string3", "string4", "string5")*

* Remember the first item is at position 0 and the final position of the range, which is the fifth position in this example, is not included.

You can also specify a **range of negative indexes** to Python Tuples, as shown in the example below:

Tuple = ("string1", "string2", "string3", "string4", "string5", "string6")
print (Tuple [-4: -2])

OUTPUT – *("string4", "string5")*

* Remember the last item is at position -1 and the final position of this range, which is the negative fourth position in this example is not included in the Output.

Unlike Python Lists, you cannot directly **change the data value of Python Tuples** after they have been created. However, conversion of a Tuple into a List and then modifying the data value of that List will allow you to subsequently create a Tuple from that updated List. Let's look at the example below:

Tuple1 = ("string1", "string2", "string3", "string4", "string5", "string6")
List1 = list (Tuple1)
List1 [2] = "update this list to create new tuple"
Tuple1 = tuple (List1)

print (Tuple1)

OUTPUT – ("string1", "string2", "update this list to create new tuple," "string4", "string5", "string6")

You can also determine the **length** of a Python Tuple using the "len()" function, as shown in the example below:

Tuple = ("string1", "string2", "string3", "string4", "string5", "string6")
print (len (Tuple))

OUTPUT – 6

You cannot selectively delete items from a Tuple, but you can use the "del" keyword to **delete the Tuple** in its entirety, as shown in the example below:

Tuple = ("string1", "string2", "string3", "string4")

del Tuple

print (Tuple)

OUTPUT – name 'Tuple' is not defined

You can **join multiple Tuples** with the use of the "+" logical operator.

Tuple1 = ("string1", "string2", "string3", "string4")
Tuple2 = (101, 202, 303)

Tuple3 = Tuple1 + Tuple2
print (Tuple3)

OUTPUT – ("string1", "string2", "string3", "string4", 101, 202, 303)

You can also use the "tuple ( )" constructor to create a Tuple, as shown in the example below:

Tuple1 = tuple (("string1", "string2", "string3", "string4"))
print (Tuple1)

EXERCISE – Create a Tuple "X" with string data values as "corn, cilantro, carrot, potato, onion" and display the item at -2 position.

USE YOUR DISCRETION HERE AND WRITE YOUR CODE FIRST

Now, check your code against the correct code below:

X = ("corn," "cilantro," "carrot," "potato," "onion")
print (X [-2])

OUTPUT – ("potato")

EXERCISE – Create a Tuple "X" with string data values as "corn, cilantro, carrot, potato, onion" and display items ranging from -1 to -3.

USE YOUR DISCRETION HERE AND WRITE YOUR CODE FIRST

Now, check your code against the correct code below:

X = ("corn," "cilantro," "carrot," "potato," "onion")
print (X [-3 : -1])

OUTPUT – ("carrot," "potato")

EXERCISE – Create a Tuple "X" with string data values as "corn, cilantro, carrot, potato, onion" and change its item from "potato" to "pepper" using List function.

USE YOUR DISCRETION HERE AND WRITE YOUR CODE FIRST

Now, check your code against the correct code below:

X = ("corn", "cilantro", "carrot", "potato", "onion")
Y = list (X)
Y [4] = "pepper"
X = tuple (Y)

print (X)

OUTPUT – (*"corn", "cilantro", "carrot", "potato", "pepper"*)

EXERCISE – Create a Tuple "X" with string data values as "corn, cilantro, carrot" and another Tuple "Y" with numeric data values as (2, 12, 22), then join them together.

USE YOUR DISCRETION HERE AND WRITE YOUR CODE FIRST

Now, check your code against the correct code below:

X = ("corn," "cilantro," "carrot")

Y = (3, 13, 23)

Z = X + Y

print (Z)

OUTPUT – ("peas," "carrots," "potato," 3, 13, 23)

Python Sets

In Python, Sets are collections of data types that cannot be organized and indexed. Sets do not allow for duplicate items and must be written within curly brackets, as shown in the syntax below.

set = {"string1", "string2", "string3"}

print (set)

Unlike the Python List and Tuple, you cannot selectively display desired items from a Set by referencing the position of that item because the Python Set are not arranged in any order. Therefore, items do not have any indexing. However, the "for" loop can be used on Sets (more on this topic later in this chapter).

Unlike Python Lists, you cannot directly **change the data values of Python Sets** after they have been created. However, you can use the "add ()" method to add a single item to Set and use the "update ( )" method to one or more items to an already existing Set. Let's look at the example below:

set = {"string1", "string2", "string3"}
set. add ("newstring")
print (set)

OUTPUT – {"string1", "string2", "string3", "newstring"}

set = {"string1", "string2", "string3"}
set. update (["newstring1", "newstring2", "newstring3",)
print (set)

OUTPUT – {"string1", "string2", "string3", "newstring1", "newstring2", "newstring3"}

You can also determine the **length** of a Python Set using the "len()" function, as shown in the example below:

set = {"string1", "string2", "string3", "string4", "string5", "string6", "string7"}
print (len(set))

OUTPUT – 7

To selectively **delete a specific item from a Set**, the "remove ( )" method can be used as shown in the code below:

set = {"string1", "string2", "string3", "string4", "string5"}
set. remove ("string4")
print (set)

OUTPUT – {"string1", "string2", "string3", "string5"}

You can also use the "discard ( )" method to delete specific items from a Set, as shown in the example below:

set = {"string1", "string2", "string3", "string4", "string5"}
set. discard ("string3")
print (set)

OUTPUT – {"string1", "string2", "string4", "string5"}

The "pop ( )" method can be used to selectively delete only the last item of a Set. It must be noted here that since the Python Sets are unordered, any item that the system deems as the last item will be removed. As a result, the output of this method will be the item that has been removed.

set = {"string1", "string2", "string3", "string4", "string5"}

A = set.pop ( )
print (A)
print (set)

OUTPUT –

String2

{"string1", "string3", "string4", "string5"}

To delete the entire Set, the "del" keyword can be used, as shown below.

set = {"string1", "string2", "string3", "string4", "string5"}
delete set
print (set)

OUTPUT – name 'set' is not defined

To delete all the items from the Set without deleting the variable itself, the "clear ()" method can be used, as shown below.

set = {"string1", "string2", "string3", "string4", "string5"}
set.clear ( )
print (set)

OUTPUT – set ( )

You can **join multiple Sets** with the use of the "union ( )" method. The output of this method will be a new Set that contains all items from both the sets. You can also use the "update ( )" method to insert all the items from one set into another without creating a new Set.

Set1 = {"string1", "string2", "string3", "string4", "string5"}
Set2 = {155, 255, 355, 455, 55}
Set3 = Set1.union (Set2)
print (Set3)

OUTPUT – {"string1", 155, "string2", 255, "string3", 355, "string4", 455, "string5", 55}

Set1 = {"string1", "string2", "string3", "string4", "string5"}
Set2 = {155, 255, 355, 455, 55}
Set1.update (Set2)
print (Set1)

OUTPUT – {255, "string1", 155, "string4", 55, "string2", 355, "string3", 455, "string5"}

You can also use the "set ( )" constructor to create a Set, as shown in the example below:

Set1 = set (("string1", "string2", "string3", "string4", "string5")) print (Set1)

OUTPUT – {"string3", "string5", "string2", "string4", "string1"}

EXERCISE – Create a Set "Veg" with string data values as "corn, cilantro, carrot, potato, onion" and add new items "pepper", "celery" and "avocado" to this Set.

USE YOUR DISCRETION HERE AND WRITE YOUR CODE FIRST

Now, check your code against the correct code below:

Veg = {"corn", "cilantro", "carrot", "potato", "onion"}
Veg.update (["pepper", "celery", "avocado"])
print (Veg)

OUTPUT – {"peas", "celery", "onion", "carrots", "broccoli", "avocado", "potato", "pepper"}

EXERCISE – Create a Set "Veg" with string data values as "corn, cilantro, carrot, potato, onion" then delete the last item from this Set.

USE YOUR DISCRETION HERE AND WRITE YOUR CODE FIRST

Now, check your code against the correct code below:

Veg = {"corn", "cilantro", "carrot", "potato", "onion"}
X = Veg.pop ( )
print (X)
print (Veg)

OUTPUT –
broccoli
{"peas", "onion", "carrots", "potato"}

EXERCISE – Create a Set "Veg" with string data values as "corn, cilantro, carrot, potato, onion" and another Set "Veg2" with items as "pepper, eggplant, celery, avocado". Then combine both these Sets to create a third new Set.

USE YOUR DISCRETION HERE AND WRITE YOUR CODE FIRST

Now, check your code against the correct code below:

Veg = {"corn", "cilantro", "carrot", "potato", "onion"}
Veg2 = {"pepper", "eggplant", "celery", "avocado"}

AllVeg = Veg.union (Veg2)   #this Set name may vary as it has not been defined in the exercise

print (AllVeg)

OUTPUT − {"peas", "celery", "onion", "carrots", "eggplant", "broccoli", "avocado", "potato", "pepper"}

Python Dictionary

In Python, Dictionaries are collections of data types that can be changed and indexed but are not arranged in any order. Each item in a Python Dictionary will comprise of a key and its value. Dictionaries do not allow for duplicate items and must be written within curly brackets, as shown in the syntax below.

dict = {
"key01": "value01",
"key02": "value02",
"key03": "value03",
}
print (dict)

You can selectively display desired item value from a Dictionary by referencing to its key inside square brackets in the print command as shown below.

```
dict = {
"key01": "value01",
"key02": "value02",
"key03": "value03",
}

X = dict ["key02"]
print (X)
```

OUTPUT – value02

You can also use the "get ( )" method to view the value of a key, as shown in the example below:

```
dict = {
"key01": "value01",
"key02": "value02",
"key03": "value03",
}

X = dict.get ("key01")
print (X)
```

OUTPUT – value01

There might be instances when you need to **change the value** of a key in a Python Dictionary. This can be accomplished by referring to the key of that item and declaring the new value. Let's look at the example below:

dict = {
"key01": "value01",
"key02": "value02",
"key03": "value03",
}

dict ["key03"] = "NEWvalue"
print (dict)

OUTPUT – {"key01": "value01", "key02": "value02", "key03": "NEWvalue"}

You can also determine the **length** of a Python Dictionary using the "len()" function, as shown in the example below:

dict = {
"key01": "value01",
"key02": "value02",
"key03": "value03",
"key4": "value4",
"key5": "value5"

}

print (len (dict))

OUTPUT – 5

Python Dictionary can also be changed by **adding** new index key and assigning a new value to that key, as shown in the example below:

dict = {
"key01": "value01",
"key02": "value02",
"key03": "value03",
}

dict ["NEWkey"] = "NEWvalue"
print (dict)

OUTPUT – {"key01": "value01", "key02": "value02", "key03": "value03", "NEWkey": "NEWvalue"}

There are multiple built-in methods to **delete items** from a Python Dictionary.

- To selectively delete a specific item value, the "pop ()" method can be used with the indicated key name.

    dict = {
    "key01": "value01",
    "key02": "value02",
    "key03": "value03",
    }
    dict.pop ("key01")
    print (dict)

    OUTPUT – { "key02": "value02", "key03": "value03"}

- To selectively delete the item value that was last inserted, the "popitem ()" method can be used with the indicated key name.

    dict = {
    "key01": "value01",
    "key02": "value02",
    "key03": "value03",
    }
    dict.popitem ( )
    print (dict)

    OUTPUT – { "key01": "value01", "key02": "value02"}

- To selectively delete a specific item value, the "del" keyword can also be used with the indicated key name.

dict = {
"key01": "value01",
"key02": "value02",
"key03": "value03",
}
del dict ("key03")
print (dict)

OUTPUT – { "key01": "value01", "key02": "value02"}

- To delete a Python Dictionary in its entirety, the "del" keyword can also be used as shown in the example below:

dict = {
"key01": "value01",
"key02": "value02",
"key03": "value03",
}
del dict
print (dict)

OUTPUT – name 'dict' is not defined

- To delete all the items from the Dictionary without deleting the Dictionary itself, the "clear ()" method can be used as shown below.

dict = {
"key01": "value01",
"key02": "value02",
"key03": "value03",
}
dict.clear ( )
print (dict)

OUTPUT – { }

There might be instances when you need to **copy** an existing Python Dictionary. This can be accomplished by using the built-in "copy ( )" method or the "dict ( )" method, as shown in the examples below:

dict = {
"key01": "value01",
"key02": "value02",
"key03": "value03",
}
newdict = dict.copy ( )

print (newdict)

OUTPUT – {"key01": "value01", "key02": "value02", "key03": "value03"}

Olddict = {
"key01": "value01",
"key02": "value02",
"key03": "value03",
}
newdict = dict (Olddict)
print (newdict)

OUTPUT – {"key01": "value01", "key02": "value02", "key03": "value03"}

There is a unique feature that supports multiple Python Dictionaries to be **nested** within another Python Dictionary. You can either create a Dictionary containing child Dictionaries, as shown in the example below:

McManiaFamilyDict = {
    "burger1" : {
        "name" : "VegWrap",
        "price" : 3.99
    },

```
        "burger2" : {
                "name" : "Burger",
                "price" : 6
        },
        "burger3" : {
                "name" : "CheeseBurger",
                "price" : 2.99
        }
}
print (McManiaFamilyDict)
```

OUTPUT - {"burger1" : { "name" : "VegWrap", "price" : 3.99}, "burger2" : {"name" : "Burger", "price" : 6}, "burger3" : {"name" : "CheeseBurger", "price" : 2.99}}

Or you can create a brand new Dictionary that contain other Dictionaries already existing on the system, your code will look like the one below:

```
burgerDict1 : {
        "name" : "VegWrap",
        "price" : 3.99
}

burgerDict2 : {
        "name" : "Burger",
```

```
        "price" : 6
}

burgerDict3 : {
        "name" : "CheeseBurger",
        "price" : 2.99
}

McManiaFamilyDict = {
        "burgerDict1" : burgerDict1,
        "burgerDict2" : burgerDict2,
        "burgerDict3" : burgerDict3
}
print (McManiaFamilyDict)
```

OUTPUT - {"burger1" : { "name" : "VegWrap", "price" : 3.99}, "burger2" : {"name" : "Burger", "price" : 6}, "burger3" : {"name" : "CheeseBurger", "price" : 2.99}}

Lastly, you can use the "dict ( )" function to create a new Python Dictionary. The key differences when you create items for the Dictionary using this function are: 1. Round brackets are used instead of the curly brackets. 2. Equal to sign is used instead of the semi-colon. Let's look at the example below:

DictwithFunction = dict (key1 = "value1", key2 = "value2", key3 = "value3")

print (DictwithFunction)

OUTPUT – {"key1": "value1", "key2": "value2", "key3": "value3"}

Python supports a large number of built-in methods that can be used on dictionaries. The table below contains all the applicable methods and its usage.

Method	Description
clear ()	Will remove all the elements from the dictionary.
copy ()	Will result in a copy of the dictionary.
fromkeys ()	Will result in a dictionary with the indicated keys and values.
get ()	Will result in the values of the indicated key.
items ()	Will result in a list containing a tuple for every key-value pair.
keys ()	Will result in a list containing the keys of the dictionary.
pop ()	Will remove the elements with the indicated key.
popitem ()	Will remove the key value pair that was most recently added.
setdefault ()	Will result in the values of the indicated key. In case the key is not found, a new key will be added with the indicated values.
update ()	Will update the dictionary with the indicated key value pairs.
values ()	Will result in a list of all the values in the dictionary.

EXERCISE – Create a Dictionary "CoffeeShop" with items containing keys as "type", "size" and "price" with corresponding values as "cappuccino", "large" and "5.99". Then add a new item with key as "syrup" and value as "caramel".

USE YOUR DISCRETION HERE AND WRITE YOUR CODE FIRST

Now, check your code against the correct code below:

CoffeeShop = {
"type" : "cappuccino",
"size" : "large",
"price" : 5.99
}
CoffeeShop ["syrup"] = "caramel"
print (CoffeeShop)

OUTPUT – {"type" : "cappuccino", "size" : "large", "price" : 5.99, "syrup" : "caramel"}

EXERCISE – Create a Dictionary "CoffeeShop" with items containing keys as "type", "size" and "price" with corresponding values as "cappuccino", "large" and "5.99". Then use a function to remove the last added item.

USE YOUR DISCRETION HERE AND WRITE YOUR CODE FIRST

Now, check your code against the correct code below:

CoffeeShop = {
"type" : "cappuccino",
"size" : "large",
"price" : 5.99
}
CoffeeShop.popitem ( )
print (CoffeeShop)

OUTPUT – {"type" : "cappuccino", "size" : "large"}

EXERCISE – Create a Dictionary "CoffeeShop" with a nested dictionary as listed below:

Dictionary Name	Key	Value
Coffee1	name	cappuccino
	size	xlarge
Coffee2	name	espresso
	size	large
Coffee3	name	mocha
	size	small

USE YOUR DISCRETION HERE AND WRITE YOUR CODE FIRST

Now, check your code against the correct code below:

```
CoffeeShop = {
        "coffee1" : {
                "name" : "cappuccino",
                "size" : "xlarge"
        },
        "coffee2" : {
                "name" : "espresso",
                "size" : "large"
        },
        "coffee3" : {
                "name" : "mocha",
                "size" : "small"
        }
}
print (CoffeeShop)
```

OUTPUT - {"coffee1" : { "name" : "cappuccino", "size" : "xlarge"}, "coffee2" : {"name" : "espresso", "size" : "large"}, "coffee3" : {"name" : "mocha", "size" : "small"}}

EXERCISE – Use the "dict ()" function to create a Dictionary "CoffeeShop" with items containing keys as "type", "size" and "price" with corresponding values as "cappuccino", "large" and "5.99".

USE YOUR DISCRETION HERE AND WRITE YOUR CODE FIRST

Now, check your code against the correct code below:

CoffeeShop = dict (type = "cappuccino", size = "large", price = 5.99}
print (CoffeeShop)

OUTPUT – {"type" : "cappuccino", "size" : "large", "price" : 5.99, "syrup" : "caramel"}

Python Classes and Objects

Python is one of the many object oriented coding languages. Every entity of Python can be considered an object and has its own methods and properties. In Python, Classes are used to construct these objects serving as object blueprints.

A Python Class can be created using the keyword "class" with a predefined property (p) as shown in the syntax below:

class ClassName:
    p = 2

A Python Object can then be created from the Python Class created above, as shown in the syntax below:

Object1 = ClassName ( )
print (object1.p)

Built-in Function

In reality, creation of classes and objects is much more complex than the basic syntax provided above. This is where a built-in function to create classes called "__init__()" is used. When the classes are being created, this inherent class function is executed with it. The "__init__()" function is mostly used for assigning values to object properties and other actions that are required for creation of an object. Let's look at the example below to understand this function:

class Vehicle:
    def __init__ (self, name, year)
    self.name = name

self.name = year

v1 = Vehicle ("BMW", 2018) __init__

print (v1.name)
print (v1.year)

OUTPUT – BMW   2018

Object Methods

There are certain methods that can be created with the Python Objects. These methods can be considered as functions of that object. For example, to create a function that would print a comment regarding ownership of the vehicle and executed on the object v1, the command below will be used:

class Vehicle:
    def __init__ (self, name, year)
    self.name = name
    self.name = year

    def newfunc (ownership):
        print ("I am a proud owner of " + self.name)

v1 = Vehicle ("BMW", 2018)

v1.newfunc ()

OUTPUT – I am a proud owner of BMW

Reference Parameter

To refer to the latest instance of a class, the "self" parameter is used. It allows you to access variables that have been derived from a class. This parameter can be named as needed and does not have to be named "self". The important thing to remember here is that the first parameter defined for a class will become the reference parameter for that class, as shown in the example below:

class Vehicle:
    def __init__ (refobject, name, year)
    refobject.name = name
    refobject.name = year

    def newfunc (xyz):
        print ("I am a proud owner of " + xyz.name)

v1 = Vehicle ("BMW", 2018)
v1.newfunc ()

OUTPUT – I am a proud owner of BMW

There might be instances when you need to **change the properties** of an object. You can easily do so by declaring the new property of the object, as shown in the example below:

class Vehicle:
    def __init__ (refobject, name, year)
    refobject.name = name
    refobject.name = year

    def newfunc (xyz):
        print ("I am a proud owner of " + xyz.name)

v1 = Vehicle ("BMW", 2018)
v1.year = 2019

You can use the "del" keyword to selectively **remove properties of an object**, as shown in the example below:

class Vehicle:
    def __init__ (refobject, name, year)
    refobject.name = name
    refobject.name = year

    def newfunc (xyz):
        print ("I am a proud owner of " + xyz.name)

v1 = Vehicle ("BMW", 2018)

del v1.year

print (v1.age)

OUTPUT – 'Vehicle' object has no 'year' attribute

You can also use the "del" keyword to entirely **delete an object**, as shown in the example below:

class Vehicle:
    def __init__ (refobject, name, year)
    refobject.name = name
    refobject.name = year

    def newfunc (xyz):
        print ("I am a proud owner of " + xyz.name)

v1 = Vehicle ("BMW", 2018)

del v1

OUTPUT – NameError: 'v1' is not defined

The "pass" statement

The definition of a Python Class must contain values or you will receive an error. However, there might be instances when the definition of a class does not have any content. In such case, you can use the "pass" statement to avoid getting an error. Look at the example below:

class Vehicle: # this class definition is empty
*   pass   # used to avoid any errors*

EXERCISE – Create a Class "CoffeeShop" with properties as "type" and "size" with corresponding values as "cappuccino" and "large" respectively.

USE YOUR DISCRETION HERE AND WRITE YOUR CODE FIRST

Now, check your code against the correct code below:

class CoffeeShop:
*   def __init__ (refobject, type, size)*
*   refobject.type = type*
*   refobject.size = size*

c1 = CoffeeShop ("cappuccino", "large")

print (c1.type)
print (c1.size)
OUTPUT – cappuccino   *large*

EXERCISE – Create a Class "CoffeeShop" with properties as "type" and "size" with corresponding values as "cappuccino" and "large" respectively. Create a new function "funct1" that would print "I would like to order a" and execute it on the object.

USE YOUR DISCRETION HERE AND WRITE YOUR CODE FIRST

Now, check your code against the correct code below:

class CoffeeShop:
    def __init__ (refobject, type, size)
    refobject.type = type
    refobject.size = size

    def funct1 (refobject):
    print ("I would like to order a" + refobject.type)

c1 = CoffeeShop ("cappuccino", "large")
c1.funct1 ( )

OUTPUT – I would like to order a cappuccino

Python Operators

In Python, a variety of Operators can be used to perform operations on a Python variable and its values. The different groups of Python operators are provided below:

Arithmetic Operators can be utilized with numerical values to execute basic math calculations.

Name	Operator	Sample
Add	+	P + Q
Subtract	-	P - Q
Multiply	*	P * Q
Divide	/	P / Q
Modulus	%	P % Q
Exponentiation	**	P ** Q
Floor division	//	P // Q

Assignment Operators can be utilized for assignment of values to a variable.

Name	Sample
=	P = 5
+=	P += 3
-=	P -= 3
*=	P *= 3
/=	P /= 3
%=	P %= 3
//=	P //= 3
**=	P **= 3
&=	P &= 3
|=	P |= 3

^=	P ^= 3
>>=	P >>= 3
<<=	P <<= 3

Comparison Operators can be utilized to draw comparison between the values.

Name	Operator	Sample
Equal	==	P == Q
Not equal	!=	P != Q
Greater than	>	P > Q
Less than	<	P < Q
Greater than or equal to	>=	P >= Q
Less than or equal to	<=	P <= Q

Logical Operators can be utilized to generate a combination of conditional statements.

Operator	Usage	Sample
and	Will return "True" if both the statements hold true.	P < 5 and P < 10
or	Will return "True" if one of the statements holds true.	P < 5 or P < 4
not	Will reverse the results and return "False" if the results are true.	not(P < 5 and P < 10)

Identity Operators can be utilized to draw a comparison between two objects to check whether the same object was created more than once using the same memory location.

Opera tor	Usage	Sample
is	Will return true if the two variables are the same object.	P is Q
is not	Will return true if the two variables are not the same object.	P is not Q

Membership Operators can be utilized to test if select sequence can be found in an object.

Operator	Usage	Sample
in	Will return True if a sequence with a specific value can be found in the object.	P in Q
not in	Will return True if a sequence with a specific value cannot be found in the object.	P not in Q

Bitwise Operators can be utilized to draw a comparison between two numeric values.

Operator	Usage	Sample
&	AND	Will set each bit to 1 if the two bits are 1

|	OR	Will set each bit to 1 if one of the two bits is 1
^	XOR	Will set each bit to 1 if only one of the two bits is 1
~	NOT	Will invert all the bits
<<	Zero fill left shift	Shifts left by pushing zero in from the right, making the left most bit to be dropped
>>	Signed right shift	Shifts right by pushing copies of the left most bit in from the left, making the right most bit to be dropped

Chapter 3: Data Visualization and Analysis with Python

Big Data

In 2001, Gartner defined Big data as "Data that contains greater variety arriving in increasing volumes and with ever-higher velocity." This led to the formulation of the "three V's". Big data refers to an avalanche of structured and unstructured data that is endlessly flooding and from a variety of endless data sources. These data sets are too large to be analyzed with traditional analytical tools and technologies but have a plethora of valuable insights hiding underneath.

The "Vs" of Big data

Volume – To be classified as big data the volume of the given data set must be substantially larger than traditional data sets. These data sets are primarily composed of unstructured data with limited structured and semi-structured data. The unstructured data or the data with unknown value can be collected from input sources such as webpages, search history, mobile applications, and social media platforms. The size and customer base of the company is usually proportional to the volume of the data acquired by the company.

Velocity – The speed at which data can be gathered and acted upon the first to the velocity of big data. Companies are increasingly using a combination of on-premise and cloud-based servers to increase the speed of their data collection. The modern-day "Smart Products and Devices" require real-time access to consumer data, in order to be able to provide them a more engaging and enhanced user experience.

Variety – Traditionally a data set would contain majority of structured data with low volume of unstructured and semi-structured data, but the advent of big data has given rise to new unstructured data types such as video, text, audio that require sophisticated tools and technologies to clean and process these data types to extract meaningful insights from them.

Veracity – Another "V" that must be considered for big data analysis is veracity. This refers to the "trustworthiness or the quality" of the data. For example, social media platforms like "Facebook" and "Twitter" with blogs and posts containing a hashtag, acronyms, and all kinds of typing errors can significantly reduce the reliability and accuracy of the data sets.

Value – Data has evolved as a currency of its own with intrinsic value. Just like traditional monetary currencies, the ultimate value of the big data is directly proportional to the insight gathered from it.

"The importance of big data doesn't revolve around how much data you have, but what you do with it. You can take data from any source and analyze it to find answers that enable 1) cost reductions, 2) time reductions, 3) new product development and optimized offerings, and 4) smart decision making."
- SAS

The functioning of big data

There are three important actions required to gain insights from big data:

Integration – The traditional data integration methods such as ETL (Extract, Transform, and Load) are incapable of collating data from a wide variety of unrelated sources and applications that are you at the heart of big data. Advanced tools and technologies are required to analyze big data sets that are exponentially larger than traditional data sets. By integrating big data from these disparate sources, companies are able to analyze and extract valuable insight to grow and maintain their businesses.

Management – Big data management can be defined as "the organization, administration, and governance of large volumes of both structured and unstructured data." Big data requires efficient and cheap storage, which can be accomplished using servers that are on-premises, cloud-based or a combination of both. Companies are able to seamlessly access required data from anywhere across the world and then processing this is a data using required processing engines on an as-needed basis. The goal is to make sure the quality of the data is high-level and can be accessed easily by the required tools and applications. Big data gathered from all kinds of Dale sources including social media platforms, search engine history and call logs. The big data usually contain large sets of unstructured data and the semi-structured data which are stored in a variety of formats. To be able to process and store this complicated data, companies require more powerful and advanced data management software beyond the traditional relational databases and data warehouse platforms.

New platforms are available in the market that is capable of combining big data with the traditional data warehouse systems in a "logical data warehousing architecture." As part of this effort, companies are required to make decisions on what data must be secured for regulatory purposes and compliance, what data must be kept for future analytical purposes, and what data has no future use and can be disposed of. This process is called "data classification," which allows a rapid and efficient analysis of a subset of data to be included in the immediate decision-making process of the company.

Analysis – Once the big data has been collected and is easily accessible, it can be analyzed using advanced analytical tools and technologies. This analysis will provide valuable insight and actionable information. Big data can be explored to make discoveries and develop data models using artificial intelligence and machine learning algorithms.

Big Data Analytics

The terms of big data and big data analytics are often used interchangeably owing to the fact that the inherent purpose of big data is to be analyzed. "Big data analytics" can be defined as a set of qualitative and quantitative methods that can be employed to examine a large amount of unstructured, structured, and semi-structured data to discover data patterns and valuable hidden insights. Big data analytics is the science of analyzing big data to collect metrics, key performance indicators, and Data trends that can be easily lost in the flood of raw data, buy using machine learning algorithms, and automated analytical techniques. The different steps involved in "big data analysis" are:

Gathering Data Requirements – It is important to understand what information or data needs to be gathered to meet the business objective and goals. Data organization is also very critical for efficient and accurate data analysis. Some of the categories in which the data can be organized are gender, age, demographics, location, ethnicity, and income. A decision must also be made on the required data types (qualitative and quantitative) and data values (can be numerical or alphanumerical) to be used for the analysis.

Gathering Data – Raw data can be collected from disparate sources such as social media platforms, computers, cameras, other software applications, company websites, and even third-party data providers. The big data analysis inherently requires large volumes of data, the majority of which is unstructured with a limited amount of structured and semi-structured data.

Data organization and categorization – Depending on the company's infrastructure Data organization could be done on a simple Excel spreadsheet or using and man tools and applications that are capable of processing statistical data. Data must be organized and categorized based on data requirements collected in step one of the big data analysis process.

Cleaning the data – to perform the big data analysis sufficiently and rapidly, it is very important to make sure the data set is void of any redundancy and errors. Only a complete data set fulfilling the Data requirements must have proceeded to the final analysis step. Preprocessing of data is required to make sure the only high-quality data is being analyzed and company resources are being put to good use.

"Big data is high-volume, and high-velocity and/or high-variety information assets that demand cost-effective, innovative forms of information processing that enable enhanced insight, decision making, and process automation."
- Gartner

Analyzing the data – Depending on the insight that is expected to be achieved by the completion of the analysis, any of the following four different types of big data analytics approach can be adopted:

- **Predictive analysis** – This type of analysis is done to generate forecasts and predictions for future plans of the company. By the completion of predictive analysis on the company's big data, the future state of the company can be more precisely predicted and derived from the current state of the company. The business executives are keenly interested in this analysis to make sure the company day-to-day operations are in line with the future vision of the company. For example, to deploy advanced analytical tools and applications in the sales division of a company, the first step is to analyze the leading source of data. Once believes source analysis has been completed, the type and number of communication channels for the sales team must be analyzed. This is followed by the use o. learning algorithms on customer data to gain ins how the existing customer base is interacting with the company's products or services. This predictive analysis will conclude with the deployment of artificial intelligence based tools to skyrocket the company's sales.

- **Prescriptive analysis** – Analysis that is carried out by primarily focusing on the business rules and recommendations to generate a selective analytical path as prescribed by the industry standards to boost company performance. The goal of this analysis is to understand the intricacies of various departments of the organization and what measures should be taken by the company to be able to gain insights from its customer data by using a prescribed analytical pathway. This allows the company to embrace domain specificity and conciseness by providing a sharp focus on its existing and future big data analytics process.

- **Descriptive analysis** – All the incoming data received and stored by the company can be analyzed to produce insightful descriptions on the basis of the results obtained. The goal of this analysis is to identify data patterns and current market trends that can be adopted by the company to grow its business. For example, credit card companies often require risk assessment results on all prospective customers to be able to make predictions on the likelihood of the customer failing to make their credit payments and make a decision whether the customer should be approved for the credit or not. This risk assessment it's primarily based on the customer's credit history but also takes into account other influencing factors, including remarks from other financial institutions that the customer had approached for credit, customer income, and financial performance as well as their digital footprint and social media profile.

- **Diagnostic analysis** – As the name suggests, this type of analysis is done to "diagnose" or understand why a certain event unfolded and how that event can be prevented from occurring in the future or replicated if needed. For example, web marketing strategies and campaigns often employ social media platforms to get publicity and increase their goodwill. Not all campaigns are as successful as expected; therefore, learning from failed campaigns is just as important, if not more. Companies can run diagnostic analysis on their campaign by collecting data pertaining to the "social media mentions" of the campaign, number of campaign page views, the average amount of time spent on the campaign page by an individual, number of social media fans and followers of the campaign, online reviews and other related metrics to understand why the campaign failed and how future campaigns can be made more effective.

The big data analysis can be conducted using one or more of the tools listed below:

- Hadoop – Open source data framework.
- Python – Programming language widely used for machine learning.
- SAS – Advanced analytical tool used primarily for big data analysis.
- Tableau – Artificial intelligence based tool used primarily for data visualization.
- SQL – the Programming language used to extract data from relational databases.
- Splunk – Analytical tool used to categorize machine-generated data
- R-programming – the Programming language used primarily for statistical computing.

Big Data Analysis vs. Data Visualization

In the wider data community, data analysis and data visualization are increasingly being used synonymously. Professional data analysts are expected to be able to skillfully represent data using visual tools and formats. On the other hand, new professional job positions called "Data visualization expert" and "data artist" have hit the market. But companies stool need professionals to analyze their data and extract valuable insights from it. As you have learned by now, Data analysis or big data analysis is an "exploratory process" with defined goals and specific questions that need to be answered from a given set of big data. Data visualization pertains to the visual representation of data, using tools as simple as an Excel spreadsheet or as advanced as dashboards created using Tableau. Business executives are always short on time and need to capture a whole lot of details. Therefore, the data analyst is required to use effective visualizations that can significantly lower the amount of time needed to understand the presented data and gather valuable insights from the data.

By developing a variety of visual presentations from the data, an analyst can view the data from different perspectives and identify potential data trends, outliers, gaps, and anything that stands out and warrants further analysis. This process is referred to as "visual analytics." Some of the widely used visual representations of the data are "dashboard reports," "infographics," and "data story." These visual representations are considered as the final deliverable from the big data analysis process but in reality, they frequently serve as a starting point for future political activities. The two completely different activities of data visualization and big data analysis are inherently related and loop into each other by serving as a starting point for as well as the endpoint of the other activity.

Data Analysis Libraries

Data Analysis libraries are sensitive routines and functions that are written in any given language. Software developers require a robust set of libraries to perform complex tasks without needing to rewrite multiple lines of code. Machine learning is largely based on mathematical optimization, probability, and statistics.

Python is the language of choice in the field of data analysis and machine learning credited to consistent development time and flexibility. It is well suited to develop sophisticated models and production engines that can be directly plugged into production systems. One of its greatest assets being an extensive set of libraries that can help researchers who are less equipped with developer knowledge to easily execute data analysis and machine learning.

"Scikit-Learn" has evolved as the gold standard for machine learning and data analysis using Python, offering a wide variety of "supervised" and "unsupervised" machine learning algorithms. It is touted as one of the most user friendly and cleanest machine learning libraries to date. For example, decision trees, clustering, linear and logistics regressions, and K-means. Scikit-learn uses a couple of basic Python libraries: NumPy and SciPy and adds a set of algorithms for data mining tasks, including classification, regression and clustering. It is also capable of implementing tasks like feature selection, transforming data and ensemble methods in only a few lines.

In 2007, David Cournapeau developed the foundational code of Scikit-Learn as part of a "Summer of code" project for "Google." Scikit-learn has become one of Python's most famous open source machine learning libraries since its launch in 2007. But it wasn't until 2010 that Scikit-Learn was released for public use. Scikit-Learn is an open sourced and BSD licensed, data mining and data analysis tool used to develop supervise and unsupervised machine learning algorithms build on Python. Scikit-learn offers machine learning algorithms, including "classification," "regression," "dimensionality reduction," and "clustering." It also offers modules for feature extraction, data processing, and model evaluation.

Designed as an extension to the "SciPy" library, Scikit-Learn is based on "NumPy" and "matplotlib," the most popular Python libraries. NumPy expands Python to support efficient operations on big arrays and multidimensional matrices. Matplotlib offers visualization tools and science computing modules are provided by SciPy. For scholarly studies, Scikit-Learn is popular because it has a well-documented, easy-to-use and flexible API. Developers are able to utilize Scikit-Learn for their experiments with various algorithms by only altering a few lines of the code. Scikit-Learn also provides a variety of training datasets, enabling developers to focus on algorithms instead of data collection and cleaning. Many of the algorithms of Scikit-Learn are quick and scalable to all but huge datasets. Scikit-learn is known for its reliability and automated tests are available for much of the library. Scikit-learn is extremely popular with beginners in machine learning to start implementing simple algorithms.

Prerequisites for application of Scikit-Learn library

The Scikit-Learn library is based on the SciPy (Scientific Python), which needs to be installed before using SciKit-Learn. This stack involves the following:

NumPy (Base n-dimensional array package)
NumPy is the basic package with Python for scientific computing. It includes among other things: "a powerful N-dimensional array object; sophisticated (broadcasting) functions; tools for integrating C/C++ and Fortran code;
Useful linear algebra, Fourier transform, and random number capabilities". NumPy is widely used as an effective multi-dimensional container of generic data in addition to its apparent scientific uses. It is possible to define arbitrary data types. This enables NumPy to integrate with a broad variety of databases seamlessly and quickly. The primary objective of NumPy is the

homogeneity of multidimensional array. It consists of an element table (generally numbers), all of which are of the same sort and are indicated by tuples of non-negative integers. The dimensions of NumPy are called "axes," and array class is called "ndarray."

SciPy (Fundamental library for scientific computing)
SciPy is a "collection of mathematical algorithms and convenience functions built on the NumPy extension of Python." It adds more impact on the interactive Python session, by offering high-level data manipulation and visualization commands and courses for the user. An interactive Python session with SciPy becomes an environment that rivals data processing and system prototyping technologies of systems such as "MATLAB, IDL, Octave, R-Lab, and SciLab."

The additional perk of basing SciPy on Python is that this also makes accessible a strong programming language for use in the development of advanced programs and specific apps. Scientific apps using SciPy benefit from developers around the globe developing extra modules in countless software landscape niches. Everything produced has been made accessible to the Python programmer, from parallel programming to web and database subroutines and classes. These powerful tools are available in addition to the mathematical libraries provided by SciPy.

IPython (Enhanced interactive console)

IPython (Interactive Python) is an interface or command shell for interactive computing using a variety of programming languages. It was originally created for the Python programming language, which supports introspection, rich media, shell syntax, tab completion, and history. Some of the features provided by IPython include: "interactive shells (terminal and Qt-based); browser-based notebook interface with code, text, math, inline plots and other media support; support for interactive data visualization and use of GUI tool kits; flexible interpreters that can be embedded to load into your own projects; tools for parallel computing."

SymPy (Symbolic mathematics)

Developed by Ondřej Čertík and Aaron Meurer, SymPy is "an open source Python library for symbolic computation." It offers algebra computing capabilities to other apps, either as a stand-alone application or as a library and even as live on the internet applications with "SymPy Live" or "SymPy Gamma." SymPy is easy to install and inspect, owing to the fact that it is completely developed in Python, boasting limited dependencies. SymPy involves characteristics ranging from calculus, algebra, discrete mathematics, and quantum physics to fundamental symbolic arithmetic. The outcome of the computations can be formatted as "LaTeX" code. Combined with a straightforward and extensible code base in a well-known language, the ease of access provided by SymPy makes it a computer algebra system with a comparatively low entry barrier.

Seaborn (data visualization) Vis Library

Seaborn is derived from the Matplotlib Library and an extremely popular visualization library. It is a high-level library that can generate specific kinds of graphs including heat maps, time series and violin plots.

Matplotlib (Comprehensive 2D/3D plotting) Vis Lb

"Matplotlib" is a 2D plotting library from Python that generates publication quality numbers across a range of hardcopy formats and interactive environments. The "Python script," the "Python" and "IPython shells," the "Jupyter notebook," the web application servers, and four user interface toolkits can be used with matplottib. Matplotlib attempts to further simplify easy tasks and make difficult tasks feasible. With only a few lines of code, you can produce tracks, histograms, power spectra, bar charts, error charts, scatter plots, etc. A MATLAB-like interface is provided for easy plotting of the Pyplot Module, especially when coupled with IPython. As a power user, you can regulate the entire line styles, font's properties and axis properties through an object-oriented interface or through a collection of features similar to the one provided to MATLAB users.

For installation of Matplotlib, either of the pip and conda files listed below are used:

"pip install matplotlib"

"conda install matplotlib"

Creation of basic graphs like linear graphs, bar charts, and histograms can be easily accomplished with the use of Matplotlib. The file below must be imported first:

"import matplotlib.pyplot as plt"

The "iris" and "wine review" dataset used in creation of the plots below using matplotlib can be imported using the pandas "read_csv" method as shown below:

"import pandas as pd
iris = pd.read_csv ('iris.csv', names= ['sepal_length', 'sepal_width', 'petal_length', 'petal_width', 'class'])
print (iris.head ())"

	sepal_length	sepal_width	petal_length	petal_width	class
0	5.1	3.5	1.4	0.2	Iris-setosa
1	4.9	3.0	1.4	0.2	Iris-setosa
2	4.7	3.2	1.3	0.2	Iris-setosa
3	4.6	3.1	1.5	0.2	Iris-setosa
4	5.0	3.6	1.4	0.2	Iris-setosa

"wine_reviews = pd.read_csv ('winemag-data-130k-v2.csv', index_col=0)
wine_reviews.head ()"

	country	description	designation	points	price	province	region_1	region_2	taster_name	taster_twitter_handle	title	variety
0	Italy	Aromas include tropical fruit, broom, brimston...	Vulkà Bianco	87	NaN	Sicily & Sardinia	Etna	NaN	Kerin O'Keefe	@kerinokeefe	Nicosia 2013 Vulkà Bianco (Etna)	White Blend
1	Portugal	This is ripe and fruity, a wine that is smooth...	Avidagos	87	15.0	Douro	NaN	NaN	Roger Voss	@vossroger	Quinta dos Avidagos 2011 Avidagos Red (Douro)	Portuguese Red
2	US	Tart and snappy, the flavors of lime flesh and...	NaN	87	14.0	Oregon	Willamette Valley	Willamette Valley	Paul Gregutt	@paulgwine	Rainstorm 2013 Pinot Gris (Willamette Valley)	Pinot Gris
3	US	Pineapple rind, lemon pith and orange blossom ...	Reserve Late Harvest	87	13.0	Michigan	Lake Michigan Shore	NaN	Alexander Peartree	NaN	St Julian 2013 Reserve Late Harvest Riesling ...	Riesling
4	US	Much like the regular bottling from 2012, this...	Vintner's Reserve Wild Child Block	87	65.0	Oregon	Willamette Valley	Willamette Valley	Paul Gregutt	@paulgwine	Sweet Cheeks 2012 Vintner's Reserve Wild Child...	Pinot Noir

Linear Graph

The "plot" method can be used to generate a linear chart in matplotlib. You will able to plot a number of columns in a single graph by looping through those desired columns and plotting them all on the same axis. Below is the sample code for the "iris" data set available on GitHub and the resulting graph for your reference.

"# getting columns to plot
columns = iris.columns.drop (['class'])
 # creation of x data
x_data = range(0, iris.shape [0])
 # creation of figure and axis
fig, ax = plt.subplots ()
 # plotting each column
for column in columns:
   ax.plot (x_data, iris[column], label=column)
 # setting title and legend
ax.set_title ('Iris Dataset')
ax.legend ()"

Histogram

The "hist" method can be used to generate a Histogram in matplotlib. The sample code below will allow passing of categorical data such as the points column from the "wine review" dataset to auto calculate the occurrences of each class.

"# creation of figure and axis
fig, ax = plt.subplots ()
 # plotting histogram
ax.hist (wine_reviews ['points'])
 # setting title and labels
ax.set_title ('Wine Review Scores')
ax.set_xlabel ('Points')
ax.set_ylabel ('Frequency')"

Bar Chart

The "bar" method can be used to generate a bar chart in matplotlib. These charts are not capable of auto calculating the occurrences of each category, so the "value_counts" function from the Pandas library needs to be used. Any set of categorical data lacking a wide variety of categories can be easily plotted using the bar chart. However, any data set containing more than 30 categories of data are too complicated to yield an easy to understand bar chart. The sample code below will allow creation of a bar chart from the "wine review" dataset using the "values_count" function.

"# creation of figure and axis
fig, ax = plt.subplots ()
 # counting the occurrence of each class
data = wine_ reviews ['points'].value_ counts()
 # getting x and y data
points = data.index
frequency = data.values
 # creation of bar chart
ax.bar (points, frequency)
 # setting title and labels
ax.set_title ('Wine Review Scores')
ax.set_xlabel ('Points')
ax.set_ylabel ('Frequency')"

Wine Review Scores

Pandas

Pandas provide highly intuitive and user-friendly high-level data structures. "Pandas" has achieved popularity in the machine learning algorithm developer community, with built-in techniques for data aggregation, grouping, and filtering as well as results of time series analysis. The Pandas library has two primary structures: one-dimensional "Series" and two-dimensional "Data Frames."

Some of the key features provided by "Pandas" are listed below:

- A quick and effective "Data Frame object" with embedded indexing to be used in data manipulation activities.
- Tools to read and write data between internal memory data structures and multiple file formats, such as "CSV" and text, "Microsoft Excel," "SQL databases," and quick "HDF5 format".

- Intelligent data alignment and integrated management of incomplete data by achieving automatic label driven computational alignment and readily manipulating unorganized data into an orderly manner.
- Flexible reconstructing and pivoting of datasets.
- Smart label-based slicing and indexing of big data sets, as well as the creation of data subsets.
- Columns can be added to and removed from data structures to achieve the desired size of the database.
- Aggregation or transformation of data using a sophisticated "Group By" system enabling execution of the "split-apply-combine" technique on the data.
- Highly efficient merge and join functions of the data set.
- "Hierarchical axis indexing" offers a simple way to work in a low dimensional data structure even with high dimensional data.
- Time-series functionalities, including "date range generation and frequency conversion, moving window statistics, moving window linear regressions, date shifting, and lagging." Also the creation of "domain-specific time offsets" and capability of joining time series with no data loss.

- Having most of the underlying code in "Cython" or "C," Pandas boasts high performance and efficiency.
- Python, in combination with Pandas, is being used in a broad range of academic and industrial sectors, including Financial Services, Statistics, Neurobiology, Economics, Marketing and Advertising, Online Data Analytics, among others.

The two types of Data Structures offered by Pandas are: "Pandas DataFrame" and "Pandas Series."

Pandas DataFrame

It is defined as "2-D labeled data structure with columns of a potentially different type". It has a high resemblance to the Excel spreadsheet, as shown in the picture below, with multiple similar features for analysis, modification, and extraction of valuable insights from the data. You can create a "Pandas DataFrame" by entering datasets from "Excel," "CSV," and "MySQL database," among others.

	NAME	AGE	DESIGNATION
1	a	20	VP
2	b	27	CEO
3	c	35	CFO
4	d	55	VP
5	e	18	VP
6	f	21	CEO
7	g	35	MD

For instance, in the picture above assume "Keys" are represented by the name of the columns and "Values" are represented by the list of items in that column, a "Python dictionary" can be used to represent this as shown in the code below:

"my_dict = {
   'name' : ["a", "b", "c", "d", "e","f", "g"],
   'age' : [20,27, 35, 55, 18, 21, 35],
   'designation': ["VP", "CEO", "CFO", "VP", "VP", "CEO", "MD"]
}"

The "Pandas DataFrame" can be created from this dictionary by using the code below:

"import Pandas as PD
df = pd.DataFrame(my_dict)"

The resulting "DataFrame" is shown in the picture below which resembles the excel spreadsheet:

	age	designation	name
0	20	VP	a
1	27	CEO	b
2	35	CFO	c
3	55	VP	d
4	18	VP	e
5	21	CEO	f
6	35	MD	g

If you would like to define index values for the rows, you will have to add the "index" parameter in the "DataFrame ( )" clause as shown below:

"df = pd.DataFrame(my_dict, index=[1,2,3,4,5,6,7])"

To obtain "string" indexes for the data instead of numeric, use the code below:

"df = pd.DataFrame(
   my_dict,
   index=["First", "Second", "Third", "Fourth", "Fifth", "Sixth", "Seventh"]
)"

Now, as these index values are uniform, you could execute the code below to utilize the "NumPy arrays" as index values:

"np_arr = np.array([10,20,30,40,50,60,70])
df = pd.DataFrame(my_dict, index=np_arr)"

Similar to "NumPy", the columns of "DataFrame" are also homogeneous. You can use dictionary like syntax or add the column name with "DataFrame", to view the data type of the column, as shown in the code below:

"df['age'].dtype   # Dict Like Syntax
df.age.dtype   # DataFrame.ColumnName
df.name.dtype   # DataFrame.ColumnName"

You can use the code below to selectively view the record or rows available within the "Pandas DataFrame," by using the "head ( )" function for the first five rows and "tail ( )" function for the last five rows. For instance, use the code below to view the first 3 rows of the data:

"df.head(3)   # Display first 3 Rows"

Pandas Series

It can be defined as a "one-dimensional labeled array capable of holding data of any type (integer, string, float, python objects)." Simply put, it is like a column in an excel spreadsheet. To generate a "Pandas Series" from an array, a "NumPy" module must be imported and used with "array ()" function, as shown in the code below:

"# import pandas as pd
import pandas as pd"

"# import numpy as np
import numpy as np"

"# simple array
data = np.array (['m','a','c','h','I','n','e'])"

"ser = pd.Series(data)
print(ser)"

Data Visualization with Scatter Plots

A scatter plot can be defined as "a two-dimensional data visualization that uses dots to represent the values obtained for two different variables-one plotted along the x-axis and the other plotted along the y-axis." It is also known as "scatter graph" or "scatter chart." For instance, the "scatter plot" seen in the picture below depicts a fictional set of height and weight measures for children. Each "dot" in the plot is used to represent an individual, with measures of their height along the "x-axis" and weight along the "y-axis."

[Scatter plot: Weight and Height of Children, with height (in) on x-axis ranging from 56 to 72 and weight (lb) on y-axis ranging from 60 to 140, showing a positive linear trend.]

"Scatter plots" are highly useful when you are interested in representing the relationship that exists between two distinct variables. "Scatter plots" are often referred to as "plots of correlation" given the fact that they demonstrate how two distinct variables are related to each other. In the "scatter plot" above, the chart depicts much more than a simple log of the height and weight of children. It also offers a visual of the relationship between the two measures, denoting that as the height increases, the child's weight is also increasing. Now, you can easily conclude that this height and weight relationship isn't ideal, as some taller kids can weigh less than some shorter kids, but the overall trend is fairly satisfactory and it can be observed that there is a direct relationship between the height and weight of children.

It is important to remember that not all relationships can be linear. For instance, the chart in the picture below indicates an "average of daily high temperature" measured over 7 years, demonstrating a familiar parabolic relationship between these variables as the daily high temperature tends to peak during summer.

Scatter plots" often contain a trend-line to clarify the relationship between the variable, as shown in the picture below.

[Weight and Height of Children scatter plot]

Moreover, the shape, size, and color of the "dot" can be considered and utilized as additional data variables. For instance, the plot below represents the data on the height and weight of the children, but by adding the color of the "dot" to depict the gender of the child, we have acquired a third variable for our analysis.

[Weight and Height of Children by Gender scatter plot]

151

Chapter 4: Machine Learning and Predictive Analysis

Machine Learning

Machine Learning can be defined as a subsidiary of artificial intelligence technology driven by the hypothesis that machines are capable of learning from data by identifying patterns and making decisions with little to no human assistance. The science of machine learning was birthed as a theory that computers have the potential to self-learn specific tasks without needing to be programmed, using the pattern recognition technique. As the machines are exposed to new data, the ability to adapt independently is the iterative aspect of machine learning. They can learn from and train themselves with prior computations to generate credible and reproducible decisions and results. The Machine learning algorithms have been in use for much longer than one would think, but their enhanced capability to analyze "big data" by automatically applying highly complex and sophisticated mathematical calculations rapidly and repeatedly has been developed recently.

Machine learning allows the analysis of large volumes of data and delivers faster and more accurate results. With proper training, this technology can allow organizations to identify profitable opportunities and business risks. Machine learning, in combination with cognitive technologies and artificial intelligence, tends to be even more effective and accurate in processing massive quantities of data. The machine learning algorithms can be categorized into four:

Supervised machine learning algorithms – These algorithms are capable of applying the lessons from the previous runs to new data set using labeled examples to successfully make predictions for the future events. For example, a machine can be programmed with data points labeled as "F" (failed) or "S" (success). The learning algorithm will receive inputs with corresponding correct outputs and run a comparison of its own actual output against the expected or correct, in an attempt to identify errors that can be fixed to make the model more efficient and accurate. With sufficient training, the algorithms are capable of providing 'targets' for any new data input through methods like regression, classification, prediction and ingredient boosting. The analysis starts from a known training data set and the machine learning algorithm then produces an "inferred function" to make future predictions pertaining to the output values. For example, supervised learning algorithm based system are smart enough to anticipate and detect the likelihood of fraudulent credit card transactions being processed.

Unsupervised machine learning algorithms – These

algorithms are used in the absence of classified and labeled training data sources. According to SAS, "Unsupervised Learning algorithms are used to study ways in which the system can infer a function to describe a hidden structure from unlabeled data i.e., to explore the data and identify some structure within." Similar to the supervised learning algorithms, these algorithms are able to explore the data and draw inferences from data sets, but cannot figure out the right output. For example, identification of individuals with similar shopping attributes, who can be segmented together and targeted with similar marketing campaigns. These algorithms are widely used to identify data outliers, provide product recommendations, and segment text topics using techniques like "singular value decomposition," "self-organizing maps," and "k-means clustering."

Semi-supervised machine learning algorithms – As the name indicates, these algorithms fall somewhere in between supervised and unsupervised learning and are capable of using labeled as well as unlabeled data as training sources. A typical training set would include the majority of the unlabeled data with a limited volume of the labeled data. The systems running on semi-supervised learning algorithms with methods such as prediction, regression and classification are able to significantly improve their learning accuracy. In situations where the acquired labeled data requires relevant and skilled resources for the machine to be able to train or learn from it, the semi-supervised learning algorithms are best suited. For example, identification of individual faces on a web camera.

Reinforcement Machine learning algorithms – These algorithms are capable of interacting with their environment by producing actions and discovering errors or rewards. The primary characteristics of reinforcement learning are trial and error research method and delayed reward. With the use of these algorithms machines can maximize its performance by automatically determining the ideal behavior within a specific context. The reinforcement signal is simply reward feedback that is required by the machine or software agents to learn which actions yield the fastest and accurate results. These algorithms are frequently used in robotics, gaming and navigation.

Applications of the machine learning technology

Virtual personal assistants
The most popular examples of virtual personal assistants are Siri and Alexa. These systems are capable of providing relevant information using simple voice commands. Machine learning is at the heart of these devices and systems, as they collect and define the information generated with every user interaction and use this information as training data to learn user preferences and provide an enhanced experience.

Predictions while driving

Most of the vehicles today are utilizing GPS navigation services, which collects information such as our current location and driving speed on a centralized server that can be used to generate a map of current traffic. This helps in managing traffic and reducing congestion. With the use of machine learning, system can estimate the regions where and the time of the day when traffic jams occur frequently. Machine learning algorithms allow ride sharing services such as Lyft and Uber, to minimize detours on their routes and provides users an upfront estimate of how much the ride will cost.

Video surveillance

Machines have taken over the monotonous job of monitoring multiple video cameras to ensure security of premises. Machines can track unusual behavior like standing motionless for an extended period of time, sleeping on benches, and stumbling. It can then send an alert to the security personnel who can make the final decision to act on the tip and avoid mishaps. With every iteration of reporting, the surveillance services are improved as the machine learning algorithms learn and improve upon itself.

Social media

Social media platforms such as "Facebook," "Twitter," and "Instagram" are using machine learning algorithms to train the system from user activity and behavior to be able to provide an engaging and enhanced user experience. Some of the examples of the functionalities that are being driven by machine learning algorithms are "People you may know" feature on Facebook (that collects and learns from user activities such as the profiles they visit often, they're own profile and their friends to suggest other Facebook users that they can become friends with) and "Similar Pins" feature on Pinterest (that is driven by computer vision Technology working in tandem with machine learning to identify objects in the images of user's saved "pins" and recommend similar "pins" accordingly).

Email spam and malware filtering

All email clients such as Gmail, Yahoo Mail and Hotmail use machine learning algorithms to ascertain that the spam filter functionality is continuously updated and cannot be penetrated by spammers and malware. Some of the spam filtering techniques that are powered by machine learning are Multi Layered Perceptron and C 4.5 decision tree induction.

Online customer service

Nowadays, most of the e-commerce sites provide users with an option to chat with a customer service representative, which is usually supported by a Chatbot instead of a live executive. These bots use machine learning technology to understand user inquiries and extract information from the website in order to be able to resolve customer issues. With every interaction, Chatbots become smarter and more humanlike.

Refinement of Search Engine Results

Search engines such as "Google," "Yahoo," and "Bing" use machine learning algorithms to provide improved search results pertinent with the user provided keywords. For every search result, the algorithm observes and learns from user activity, such as opening suggested links and the order in which the opened link was displayed as well as time spent on the opened link. This helps the search engine to understand which search results more optimal and any modifications needed to further improve the search results.

Product recommendations

The product recommendation feature has now become the heart and soul of online shopping experience. Machine learning algorithms in combination with artificial intelligence fuel the product recommendation functionality. The system observes and learns from consumer activity and behavior such as past purchases, wish list, recently viewed items, and liked or added to cart items.

Online fraud detection

The financial institutions are relying heavily on machine learning algorithms and artificial intelligence to make cyber space secure by tracking potentially fraudulent monetary transactions online.

For example, PayPal is using Machine learning algorithms to prevent money laundering through its platform. They're using a set of artificial intelligence tools in combination with Machine learning algorithms to analyze millions of transactions and distinguish between legitimate and illegitimate transactions between the buyer and the seller. With every transaction, the system learns which transactions are legitimate and which transactions could be potentially fraudulent.

Predictive Analytics

According to SAS, predictive analytics is *"use of data, statistical algorithms, and machine learning techniques to identify the likelihood of future outcomes based on historical data. The goal is to go beyond knowing what has happened to providing a best assessment of what will happen in the future"*. Today companies are digging through their past with an eye on the future and this is where artificial intelligence for marketing comes into play, with the application of predictive analytics technology. The success of predictive analytics is directly proportional to the quality of big data collected by the company.

Here are some of the widely used predictive analytics applications for marketing:

Predictive analysis for customer behavior

For the industrial giants like "Amazon," "Apple," and "Netflix," analyzing customer activities and behavior is fundamental to their day to day operations. Smaller businesses are increasingly following in their footsteps to implement predictive analysis in their business model. The development of a customized suite of predictive models for a company is not only capital-intensive but also requires extensive manpower and time. Marketing companies like "AgilOne" offer relatively simple predictive model types with wide applicability across industrial domains. They have identified three main types of predictive models to analyze customer behavior, which are:

"Propensity models" – These models are used to generate "true or accurate" predictions for customer behavior. Some of the most common propensity models include: "predictive lifetime value," "propensity to buy," "propensity to turn," "propensity to convert," "likelihood of engagement," and "propensity to unsubscribe."

"Cluster models" – These models are used to separate and group customers based on shared attributes such as gender, age, purchase history, and demographics. Some of the most common cluster models include: "product based or category base clustering," "behavioral customs clustering," and "brand based clustering."

"Collaborative filtering" – These models are used to generate products and services and recommendations as well as to recommended advertisements based on prior customer activities and behaviors. Some of the most common collaborative filtering models include: "up sell," "cross sell," and "next sell" recommendations.

The most significant tool used by companies to execute predictive analytics on customer behavior is "regression analysis," which allows the company to establish correlations between the sale of a particular product and the specific attributes displayed by the purchasing customer. This is achieved by employing "regression coefficients," which are numeric values depicting the degree to which the customer behavior is affected by different variables, and developing a "likelihood score" for future sale of the product.

Qualification and Prioritization of Leads

There are three primary categories employed in business to business or B2B predictive analytics marketing to qualify and prioritize prospective customers or "leads." These categories are: **"Predictive scoring"** which is used to prioritize prospective customers on the basis of their likelihood to make an actual purchase

"**Identification models**" which are used to identify and acquire new prospective customers on the basis of attributes that are shared with the existing customers of the company.

"**Automated segmentation,**" which is used to separate and classify prospective customers on the basis of shared attributes to be targeted with the same personalized marketing strategies and campaigns.

The predictive analytics technology needs a large volume of sales data that serves as a building block and training material to increase the accuracy and efficiency of the predictive models. Small brick-and-mortar companies cannot afford to expand their computing resources. Therefore, are unable to efficiently collect customer behavioral data from their in-store sales. This translates into a competitive edge for larger companies with more advanced computing system, which exacerbates the superfluous growth of larger companies in comparison to small businesses.

Identification of current market trends

Companies can employ "data visualization" tools that allow business executives and managers to gather insights on the current state of the company, simply by visualizing their existing customer behavioral data on a "report or dashboard." These dashboard reports tend to inspire and generate customer behavior driven actions. For example, with the use of data visualization tools, a company can identify the underlying trend of customer demands in specific neighborhoods and accordingly plan to stock their inventory for individual stores. The same information can bring to light the best products and services for the company to be launched on the basis of the current market trends that can suffice the customer demands. The market trend insights can also be applied to increase the efficiency of the company's supply chain management model.

Customer segmentation and targeting

One of the simplest and highly effective way of optimizing a product offer to achieve a rapid turnaround on the company's return on investment is the ability to target "right customers" with appropriate product offers at the "right time." This also happens to be the most common and widely used application of predictive analytics in the world of marketing. According to a research study conducted by the "Aberdeen Group," companies using predictive analytics in their marketing strategies are two times more likely to successfully identify "high value customers." This is where the quality of company's existing data set takes precedence. The highly recommended practice is to use historical consumer behavioral data of all existing customers and analyze it to segment and target customers with similar purchasing attributes with a personalized recommendations and marketing campaigns.

Some of the most common predictive analytics models used, and this application are "affinity analysis," "churn analysis," and "response modeling." Using these applications, companies can gather insight such as "if combining digital and print subscriptions of their product offerings or catalog is a good idea" or "whether their product or service will be more successful if offered as a monthly subscription model or one time purchase fee." One of the leading sales and marketing platform companies is "Salesforce," which offers a cloud based platform that can be used by businesses to generate customer profiles as a product of the data collected from independent sources, including customer relationship management (CRM) applications and other company applications. By selectively and mindfully adding inputted data to this platform, companies can seamlessly track their customer behavior to develop a customer behavioral model overtime that can feed into company's decision-making process in real time and over the long term.

Development of marketing strategies

Another application of predictive analytics and marketing is providing access to a variety of customer related data such as data collected from social media platforms and companies own internal structured data. The customer behavioral model can then be generated by collating all available data and applying "behavioral scoring" on it. All the companies across different industrial sectors are required to adapt to changing or evolving customer behavior through proliferating marketing mediums or channels. For example, companies can use any of the predictive analytics model described above, to precisely predict if their planned marketing campaign would have more success on the social media platforms or on their mobile applications.

Companies are able to employ predictive analytics model to gain an understanding of how their customers are interacting with their products or services based on their feelings or emotions shared on the social media platforms concerning a particular topic. This process is referred to as "sentiment analysis" or "text analysis."

Exploratory analysis of customer data

"Exploratory Data Analysis" or EDA provides a comprehensive view of existing customer data generated pertinent customer data sources such as product prices, current and historical customer surveys, product usage, purchase history, and demographics. It is considered as an approach to look at the data without the use of any statistical model and the data inferences. The term "Exploratory Data Analysis" was coined by John Tukey, in his book released in 1977. Some of the main reasons to use exploratory data analysis are:

- Preliminary selection of the applicable "predictive models."
- Verification of underlying assumptions.
- Make sure the company is asking the right questions to expand its customer base.
- Detect potential data anomalies, redundancies and errors.
- Determination of the relationship between the "explanatory variables."
- Assessment of the direction and size of the relationship between "explanatory variables" and "outcome variables."

The customer data collected in the database form of a rectangular array with individual columns for "subject identifier," "outcome variable" and "explanatory variable." It is rather challenging to look at a spreadsheet filled with numerical values and determine important information from the data and this is where exploratory data analysis techniques are used to selectively display important character is to of the data. There are four types of exploratory data analysis techniques:

1. **"Univariate non-graphical"** - This technique looks at a single variable or data column at a time and displays the results as a statistical summary.

2. **"Multivariate non- graphical"** - This technique looks at two or more variables or data columns at a time and displays the results as a statistical summary.
3. **"Univariate graphical"** - This technique looks at a single variable or data column at a time and displays the results diagrammatically or using pictorial graphs.
4. **"Multivariate graphical"** - This technique looks at two or more variables or data columns at a time and displays the results diagrammatically or using pictorial graphs.

EDA helps in the determination of the best predictive model to address the business problem by generating a low risk and low cost comprehensive report of the data findings and solution recommendations for best suited customer data models. The in-depth exploratory analysis of customer behavior provides exposure to hidden data patterns and market trends that would have been easily lost in the mass of information. Some of the conclusions that can be derived using EDA on customer behavioral data are:

- Identification of customers with the highest number of purchases and the maximum amount of money spent.
- Finding the number of orders generated on a daily, weekly, and monthly basis.
- Identification of the distribution of the unit price for all company products.

- Identify purchase transaction patterns based on demographics and location of the customers.

Personalized marketing with Artificial Intelligence

In a research study sponsored by "Researchscape International," about 75% of the marketing agencies stated that personalize marketing has immensely held their companies and clients in advancing customer relationships, and a whopping 97% stated that they will continue to invest in personalized marketing efforts. This is primarily driven by the fact that companies are able to effectively communicate with their target markets by gathering valuable insights from customer behavioral data using predictive analytics and machine learning algorithms. Typically, personalization starts from an individual customer but can potentially be applied to a segment of customers with shared attributes and achieve "personalization at scale." Artificial intelligence based tools and applications can perform image recognition and voice analysis in combination with customer behavior analysis to provide companies a deeper understanding of customer demands and needs that can be met by delivering precise product recommendations.

Here are some industrial applications of personalized marketing:

Ad targeting

Companies can target advertisements to a specific user or a segment of customers based on their shopping attributes such as recent views of a particular product or category and purchase history. Some of the Ad targeting applications available in the market are:

"ReFUEL4" – The "Ad Analyzer," developed by the marketing company "ReFUEL4", utilizes computer's visual capabilities to predict the performance of the advertisement. If the company's existing ad starts declining in performance, the ad analyzer can help the company to develop a new and better ad. The decline in ad performance typically signals audience fatigue, when people stop paying attention to the ad because it has become too familiar and uninteresting.

"Match2one" – This advertising application can be integrated into the company's e-commerce site and used to I've tracked prospective customers and retain existing customers. The "Match2One" application uses machine learning algorithms to target potential customers that have a higher likelihood of paying consumers. The company claims that it's "engine is trained to generate leads and find new customers using a combination of site visitor behavior and historical data." By analyzing the website visitor data, the application can show targeted ads to the customers hold displayed interest and in particular product.

Personalized messaging

The most important aspect of personalized messaging is contextual marketing. To make sure relevant messages are being sent to the target audience, companies gather customer data, including their behavior, webpage view history, preferred content, social media posts, and demographics, among other variables. Some of the personalized messaging application available in the market are:

"Dynamic yield" – The email solution provided by the company uses customer behavioral data such as order history, email clicks, social media activity, among other features to generate personalized email content for the individual customers. The email solution supplies dynamic email templates that can be easily customized to reflect relevant messages. This application is used across several industrial domains, including travel, E-commerce, gaming industry and social media.

"Yoochoose" – This company offers e-commerce services to online retailers that allows the company to create a "personalized shopping experience" for their consumers, using personalized emails or targeted notifications with newsletters and product recommendations that automatically triggered buy customer behavior. The application is capable of identifying customers who have not made a purchase for some time and trigger a notification to remind them to make a purchase. It can also identify customers who have recently made a purchase and trigger an "after sale, thank you" email. The company offers the "target notifications" functionality along with a product recommendation engine and a "personalized search," all of which are packaged into a "personalization suite."

Product recommendations

The easiest and smartest read for any company to grow their business is to provide accurate product recommendations that are relevant to the needs and demands of the customer. Companies can also reduce the volume and frequency of product returns while increasing their income through new products, repeat purchases and retargeting to entice new potential customers and higher customer loyalty. Some of the product recommendations applications available in the market are:

"Recombee" – This application is based on advance machine learning algorithms that are capable of generating recommendations within "200 millisecond of the customer activity". The company claims that its application can generate over 500 recommendations per second, by employing a combination of "collaborative filtering algorithms" developed for customer behavioral analysis and "content based algorithms" to analyze product titles and descriptions. With every human interaction, the learning algorithms improves upon itself and continues to refine the recommendations with iterative use by the customer. This application is widely used in real estate industry, job boards, classified ad, gaming industry, travel industry and entertainment industry, among others.

"Sentient Aware" – The product recommendation engine offered by "Sentient Aware" analyzes consumer's Visual activity and behavioral interactions to activate the "deep learning algorithms" within the company website. This application utilizes "intent and curation driven algorithms" to identify similar products and the company catalog to generate predictions on customers Preferences and make product recommendations that align with those preferences. The company claims that its application is just as efficient at recommending products for first-time users owing to its capability to generate recommendations without using historical data.

Dynamic websites

A website that can cater to individual site preferences of every customer on-the-fly by dynamically changing its content, which is driven by underlying scripts, is called a "dynamic website." The repetitive tasks including tagging photos and rendering photos, are carried out using artificial intelligence technologies such as "image recognition" and "machine learning." Some of the dynamic website applications available in the market today are:

"Bookmark" – The company "Bookmark" has successfully applied Machine learning technology to web design. The company claims that its "AI Design Assistant" or (AIDA) can custom build company websites pertaining to various website elements, sections and images as well as the overall web design that should feature on the site based on the company's industry specific information. "AIDA" is capable of searching the Internet to gather more information about the client company by running a search on the company name location and type of business. This application collects information on client's customer behavior and activity on social media and analyzes that information to determine the best website elements and design for the company's e-commerce platform.

"LiftIgniter" –The dynamic website recommendation system developed by "LiftIgniter," can be directly integrated with the client's e-commerce platforms online and on mobile applications and is driven by the machine learning algorithm called "true parallel multivariate algorithms infrastructure." This integrated system learns from the customer interactions with the e-commerce platforms and sifts through all of company's online content to display recommended products within 150 milliseconds that the customer might be interested in based on their real time activity on the platform.

Conclusion

Thank you for making it through to the end of *Python for Data Science: A Python Crash Course for Data Science, Data Analysis, Python Machine Learning, and Big Data*, let's hope it was informative and able to provide you with all of the tools you need to achieve your goals whatever they may be.

The next step is to make the best use of your new-found wisdom of Python programming, data science, data analysis, and machine learning that have resulted in the birth of the powerhouse, which is the "Silicon Valley." Businesses across the industrial spectrum with an eye on the future are gradually turning into big technology companies under the shadow of their intended business model. This has been proven with the rise of the "FinTech" industry attributed to the financial institutions and enterprises across the world. This book is filled with real-life examples to help you understand the nitty-gritty of the underlying concepts along with the names and descriptions of multiple tools that you can further explore and selectively implement to make sound choices for the development of a desired machine learning model. Now that you have finished reading this book and mastered the use of Python programming, you are all set to start developing your own Python based machine learning model as well as performing big data analysis using all the open sources readily available and explicitly described in this book. You can position yourself to use your deep knowledge and understanding of all the cutting edge technologies obtained from this book to contribute to the growth of any company and land yourself a new high paying and rewarding job!

Finally, if you found this book useful in any way, a review on Amazon is always appreciated!

Made in the USA
Middletown, DE
01 February 2020